Strange Hwy

Short Stories

Strange Hwy

Short Stories

Beem Weeks

Fresh Ink Group
Guntersville

Strange Hwy
Short Stories

Fresh Ink Group
An Imprint of:
The Fresh Ink Group, LLC
Box 931
Guntersville, AL 35976
Email: info@FreshInkGroup.com
FreshInkGroup.com

Edition 1.0 2018

Book design by Amit Dey / FIG

Cover by Stephen Geez / FIG

Cataloging-in-Publication Recommendations:
FIC029000 **FICTION** / Short Stories (single author)
FIC043000 **FICTION** / Coming of Age
FIC019000 **FICTION** / Literary

Library of Congress Control Number: 2018963266

ISBN-13: 978-1-947867-39-0 Papercover
ISBN-13: 978-1-947867-38-3 Hardcover
ISBN-13: 978-1-947867-40-6 Ebooks

Table of Contents

To the memory of
Ann Stewart and Jan Hawke

Acknowledgements

Shirley Michael; Lisa Walworth; Darin Weeks; Brook Krieger; Stephen Geez; Fresh Ink Group; Dennis Glover; Cloudsgrey (Kelly Jean Rice); and to Nonnie Jules and the entire Rave Reviews Book Club community

ACKNOWLEDGEMENTS

[illegible] Weaver, [illegible] Kruger, [illegible] Dennis Glover, [illegible] and the [illegible] Book Club community.

STRANGE HWY
Short Stories

Alterations

In the summer of 1959, the summer before the start of my ninth-grade year, I, Madeline Penny, killed my father. Not directly, mind you. But sometimes even indirectly makes a person just as guilty as if she'd pulled the trigger herself.

* * *

I heard them talking in their backyard, the man and the girl—his daughter, perhaps? Their language resembled gibberish, certainly nothing I could grab hold of and uncover any specific meaning behind the sound. They'd only just moved into the house next to ours the day before.

My father caught me listening, straining to hear from our side of the fence. "They're Russians," he said, stepping out onto the patio, his after-work martini in hand. "And boy is the brass at the Yard in a real tizzy!"

The *Yard* meant the Connor-Wells Ship Yard, where my father worked. Dad didn't build the ships; he made sure they got built the way Uncle Sam wanted them built.

"Why are they here?" I asked, dropping onto the lawn chair opposite the one my father claimed.

His shoulders twitched that uptight shrug he resorted to whenever he didn't know the answer to a question that rang simple.

"I heard piano over there," I said, sliding closer to him, hoping for a sip from that martini. "Really good piano—the kind like that man played at the New Year's dance."

"Jazz," my father sighed, handing over the nearly empty glass. "Don't let your mother smell that on your breath."

* * *

One of two things usually happened whenever my father arrived home after work: Either my mother would take his briefcase and hand him a martini, or he'd keep the briefcase and disappear into his office for an hour or two. The latter meant nobody but my father carried clearance to handle the briefcase with its kept secrets.

This night, there'd been no secrets to secure.

"Piano," my mother told my father, passing the mashed potatoes around the table. "*Jazz* piano. I heard several Brubeck pieces—sounded just like the recordings."

My father nodded, accepting the bowl of spuds. "Perhaps that's all you heard—recordings, I mean."

My mother ignored Daddy's assumption, pushed forward with her own notions. "I'm wondering if he teaches," she said. "Wouldn't it be lovely if Maddie had a proper teacher again?"

"How do you know it's not *her?*" I argued, knowing full well the girl I saw probably made all that music.

But my mother had a way of seeing more than my eyes ever did. "I caught her on the patio—smoking cigarettes, no less—while the music played."

* * *

That's where I met the girl—on their patio, smoking a cigarette, two nights later.

"And what is *your* name, Miss Nosy One?" she asked, her voice thick with accent—Russian, most certainly.

I wasn't really on *their* patio. I just sort of peered over the fence. "Madeline," I informed the tall girl. "But everybody just calls me Maddie."

"Why? If your name is called Madeline, why do they not call you Madeline?"

I gave her my father's uptight shrug. "What do they call *you?*"

"Masha," she answered. And if anybody ever called her anything else, she'd have her say in the matter.

"I play piano," I blurted, hoping to settle onto some common ground with this girl.

But Masha didn't care. "You want cookie for this?"

* * *

I didn't see her again for another week, though I'm quite certain she didn't ever leave her house. The second time we met I walked around the fence and stood there beside her while she chain-smoked Winston cigarettes and mumbled bits of conversation in her mother tongue.

"Why you bother me?" she asked, stepping on a spent butt. "I need friend, you think?"

She could have been any one of those girls in the teen magazines—the pretty ones who never long for attention from boys. She called to mind Grace Kelly—but only in looks, with her short blond hair and big blue eyes. Masha smoked like a man and spoke poorly—though I blamed that on the fact English wasn't her first language.

"Be friendly," my mom told me one night after dinner. "The poor thing doesn't appear to have a mother."

The girl began to warm to me after a few short backyard patio visits. She even shared a cigarette with me once. She took a drag, handed it over, said, "You come over some night, we play records." Gave it like an order, she did.

I managed a short nod, asked, "What kind of music do you listen to?"

"Buddy Holly, mostly—since he die."

Masha wasn't much older than me. Two years, I'd guess—three tops. Still, at that age, most girls won't bother hanging with someone younger. I know I wouldn't waste a minute of time hanging around some runny-nosed fourth- or fifth-grader.

"Elvis," I said. "I'm an Elvis girl."

Dismissive, that gesture she made with her hand. "No Elvis on *my* record player; only Buddy Holly—and Little Richard, too."

"What have you got against Elvis?" I demanded to know the source of this outrage.

That dismissive gesture reappeared, settling her side of the matter without a spoken word.

* * *

It felt just like home, that first time I entered Masha's house. The layout mirrored my own family's dwelling place.

A Steinway filled half of the small living room. Sheet music spilled from a loose pile atop the piano. No television to be found.

"He's quite good, your father," I told her, eyeing the instrument. "I've heard him a few times. My mother thinks he's as good as Dave Brubeck."

Masha's cool blue gaze wandered the length of me, giving off a distinct disapproval of the poodle skirt, white blouse, and saddle shoes I'd chosen to wear. "Why you think he's my father?" she asked.

"You live here with him, don't you?"

"Could be he's my lover, no?"

"No!" I assured her. "You aren't old enough for that sort of thing."

"In Russia, these things happen all the time."

"This isn't Russia."

A smile, delicate in its beauty, teased the corners of her mouth. "Okay, so he's my father. You like that better?"

I didn't. Maybe I suddenly preferred her version—and the danger that goes with it.

In the kitchen, set up just like my mother's, Masha plopped down at the table, motioned for me to take the seat across from her. "I make you martini, yes?" she asked.

Okay, so that grin on my lips didn't mean I'd agree. But truly, I really began to like this girl—a lot! "We're not old enough for martinis," I said, hoping she'd push it until I gave in.

"You drink from your father's glass. I see this every night."

True. But that's only a swallow or two. I'd never had a full drink to myself.

Her hand went dismissive again. "Maybe you stay over some night—then we have martini and cigarettes and Buddy Holly music, yes?"

* * *

My father and his briefcase vanished behind his office door for most of the night. He didn't even bother coming out for dinner.

"Submarines," my mother explained. "They're building a new model at the yard—or at least that's the hope."

This meant my father would be gone most of the time, working long hours into the night, leaving me and my mother to get by without his company at dinner. He'd miss our favorite television shows, too. But I'd watch and fill him in on the silly antics of Beaver Cleaver or the goings on with *The Real McCoys*. I'd grown accustomed to these periodic absences.

* * *

"We go to beach," Masha said, standing on my front porch. "You come, too?"

Over her shoulder stood the one I figured to be her father. Up close and in the midday sun he appeared far too young to have a teenage daughter. Tall and wiry, he was, with a mess of black hair that gave him an air of suspicion.

Dangerous, my mother would say—just not today.

"Of course Maddie may go to the beach with you," my mother said, inviting the two inside. Almost immediately she started on with her piano talk. How long has he played? Does he perform recitals? Does he teach?

I slipped into my bedroom, went about changing into my pink one-piece. But Masha wouldn't have any of it.

"You fit this?" she asked, holding out a white two-piece.

A *bikini!*

"My mother won't allow *that*," I assured her.

"Wear it under shorts and shirt."

Masha watched me undress down to my birthday suit, eyed me like maybe she had opinions she intended to make known. She didn't utter a word, though; she just smiled that delicate thing I'd grown used to seeing whenever she got her way.

* * *

She never once called him Dad or Father. Masha always addressed the man as Victor. She smoked in front of him without fear of repercussion. They spoke back and forth in Russian, occasionally tossing glances at me, riding alone in the back seat.

Being with Masha felt like a new-found freedom I'd never known before. Nothing would be off limits with her around.

Boys stared—mostly at her—as we searched out a place to spread our towels on the crowded beach. Masha had the sort of body for which the bikini was designed—long and leggy, full breasts just demanding attention in that skimpy top, a perfect bottom.

But even as Masha drifted away to dip her toes into the cool Pacific, many of those staring eyes remained on me.

"You are pretty girl," Victor announced, lying on the beach towel beside mine.

I gave him one of Masha's dismissive hand gestures.

He said, "Every boy here look at you. Every boy here want you."

Couldn't argue with that—the looking part, at least. I can't say for sure what all went on inside the minds behind all those staring eyes; I just knew I liked the attention. Boys didn't normally bother with me.

Victor propped himself on his elbow, said, "Masha say you like martini, yes?"

My head gave up a nod. "Martini is my father's favorite."

"Perhaps we have one tonight, yes?"

I'd love one. But my mother would smell it on my breath the moment I walked through the front door—and I told him as much.

Masha wandered into our conversation, told of her aunt with a house just off the beach. "You call your mother," she explained. "We stay tonight."

Victor's blue gaze pierced my soul, dared my consent. "We have big fun, yes? No worry your mother find out." He wore those loose shorts all the surfers wear, though he didn't look anything like an actual surfer.

Before I could count the reasons why I needed to be home tonight, my head nodded consent.

* * *

Of course my mother agreed I could stay the night. Victor had yet to commit to taking me on as a student—let him get to know me better. To my mother, learning piano from a Russian teacher represented the perfect addition to the résumé I'd need to get into Berklee or Juilliard or wherever she imagined.

Katerina looked nothing at all like Victor. If she truly were an aunt to Masha, it had to be on her mother's side. Katerina stood taller than Victor by half a foot. Where he had those dark curls, hers fell straight and blond.

Boys were there, as well—two of them, both speaking Russian.

Martinis were mixed, music blared from the hi-fi. Masha played Buddy Holly and Dion and Ricky Nelson, while disregarding Victor's requests for Brubeck and Miles Davis.

* * *

I'd never had a full martini before—let alone two. The alcohol pooled inside my brain, just behind my eyes. Laughter and dancing turned into lethargy. My feet went heavy. The room tilted like a carnival funhouse. My head took on the weight of an over-sized pumpkin and tipped forward as if I intended to fall asleep right there on the sofa . . . where I dropped.

* * *

I don't recall being carried away to that tiny bedroom at the back of the house; I just ended up in there. Darkness obscured the one kissing me, the one belonging to those hands that searched out secrets they lacked clearance to know. But it's my own will that bent, that granted permission. I'm the one who gave in to that boy speaking Russian.

* * *

My mother's the one who figured it out. The doctor just confirmed the matter two months later. But by then, Victor and Masha had disappeared into the vastness of the world, just out of reach of those seeking justice on my behalf.

"They did this to us," my father lamented. "Ruined us, they did."

There weren't many single teenage mothers in 1959. Society wouldn't tolerate such blatant show of disregard for proper behavior.

Minnesota became my home for the next seven months, out there where my father's sister could keep me hidden away from nosy speculations. It's there that I received the news that forever altered my life.

The brass at the shipyard, upon finding out about my predicament—and the potential connection to the Russians—determined that my father could no longer be trusted with a high-level clearance from Uncle Sam. His dismissal proved more than he could handle. One night, while my mother slept, my father drove to a quiet park near our home, put a gun in his mouth, and pulled the trigger.

* * *

I gave birth to a baby boy that I never got to hold or see. A family from Minneapolis took him away and did the job of raising him.

I returned to my mother, who'd since rented an apartment in Sacramento. She took a job as secretary in a law firm, eventually marrying an attorney.

Me? I graduated on time—with honors. I drifted toward San Francisco after turning down a scholarship for San Jose State University. Minneapolis lingered in the shadows behind my eyes. I never went, though. It wouldn't be right to disrupt something of which I could never be a part.

In 1966 I met a man at a Beatles concert in Candlestick Park. We married a year later, and together we raised two boys and a girl. Life got good again.

But that notion would always remain with me. It would always remind me of what I knew deep in my heart.

I killed my father.

He's just the one who pulled the trigger.

Constant as the Day

It's what your grandmother used to say: Constant as the day. You probably don't remember that, though. She died before you were old enough to appreciate her wisdom. It just means that certain things in life will never change—no matter the consequences.

I saw you go in there this afternoon, into your bedroom closet, the way you've done a thousand times before. This time was different. The air lacked its charge, that spark your presence always added. I guess I expected this moment—God knows most of the family had already accepted it. But acceptance doesn't come easy to a mother.

That you'd be the one to deny me grandchildren—*that* had been established long ago. I know, I have three other children. There will be plenty of little ones running around the house again one day. It's just so far from what I imagined for you.

I always blamed myself—though deep inside I know it's not my fault. Did I neglect you in some way? Is the divorce the determining factor in the road you chose? Just remember, your *father* left *us*. I didn't have a say in that decision.

Still, here we are.

You lie on the floor inside the closet, the way you've done since childhood, when you'd sneak inside and fall asleep. I remember the frantic search that first time. We scoured the house and the yard looking for you. Nobody thought to peer inside the closet. Maybe we'd been subconsciously afraid of the bones we hoped would remain hidden.

It's there beside you, that dirty spoon and stub of a candle. You didn't even last long enough to pull the needle from your arm. At first I saw those as tools of the devil. Those were the things that changed you from a happy little girl into the brooding young woman so filled with darkness. It didn't happen overnight, though.

The pallor of your skin is highlighted by the deep purple where blood has pooled against your left cheek, the telltale sign it no longer flows through your body, keeping you warm, keeping you alive. Everything for you has stopped: your heart, your mind, your potential.

Not to sound morbid, but I pictured this moment a hundred times over the years. Even before I touch your face I know what awaits my fingertips.

The first time you overdosed I blamed myself. The second time, I blamed God. The third time, well, I realized that God was just as sad as me. It's why I always looked in on you, seeing you on the closet floor. I'd count the times your chest would rise and fall in a minute, hoping that one minute would lead to a second, then to another, until you'd open your eyes.

I don't know what happened today. Or maybe I do know. Either way, I just couldn't look in on you this time. I didn't have it in me to count one more minute.

I made plans for you. I know, you had your own ideas. But mine were better, healthier. My plans saw you falling in love with a nice boy, a boy you'd want to hold on to forever. I used to think Jeffrey Kellen might be that boy, the way you used to look at him whenever he'd happen by the house—always at dinner time. But then he went away—Iraq, as I recall. When he returned home in that bag, I just knew that was probably it for you. You were just too delicate to cope with another loss so close on the heels of your father's leaving us.

I hate that you're cold now and there's nothing I can do to warm your body. You just don't understand how unnatural this moment is for a mother. I hate you as much as I love you.

I wasn't a mother until you. And you weren't expected, either. No, ma'am. Your father and I, we had no intention of parenthood so soon into our marriage. We'd planned the first ten years of our time together—the way musicians plot out their intended rise to world domination. We were meant to see Europe, Asia, maybe hit the lower forty-eight. But then you changed all that—to the delight of my mother. Then came the other three; and your father, he decided he was still young enough to do Europe—with the babysitter.

You don't look like you. Not now. The soul is gone, and all that remains is a shell, a husk, a thing to be discarded, moved away like some secret family shame meant to stay hidden.

Inside your closet I crouch beside you, stroking your hair, tracing your cold lips with the tips of my fingers, the way I did when you were two and three and four years old and couldn't—or wouldn't—fall asleep. It used to drive your father crazy. "Just leave her be," he'd argue. "She'll get tired on her own." He was in love with me back then. He saw you as a sort of competitor, a threat to his time alone with me.

I would have died for you.

But you wouldn't let me.

That you've broken my heart is a given. But that's the curse of parenthood. We give you life, invent notions of what and who you'll be; and you turn our worlds upside down, becoming a junkie without aim, without reason, without a thought for what you've done to us—to me.

I resent you for the call I must make. What am I supposed to say to those people? How do I phrase such a conversation? Do I say, "Hello? My oldest child has passed away from an overdose. Would you please come and retrieve the body before her siblings get home from school?"

The thing that amazes me the most is the calm tone of my own voice as I say those very words into my cell phone. It's almost a matter-of-fact discussion between me and the woman on the other end.

"Lynnette," I say, when they ask the name of my deceased child. "Lynnette Grace Priner. We named her after my mother and her father's sister."

They care nothing for the intimate details of your existence.

"Heroin," I explain, when they ask of a potential cause for your demise. "We tried rehab—twice."

Again, this last bit of information means nothing to the voice on the other end of this conversation.

Twenty-one years—that's all we'll know of you in this world.

I want to cry—I *need* to cry—but that's just not happening today. Not now, at least. You've drained me of my tears since that first time I knew you'd chosen this path. I just don't have it in me to shed one more.

Perhaps when we put you in the ground . . .

I'll miss you—the way a parent ought to miss a lost child. But I will not be bound by emotional necessities. You're gone and nothing can bring you back. Please don't think me cruel, but I am alive. I am resurrected from the grave. I need no longer pine for a wayward daughter. Nothing more can happen to you in this world. Your death is my salvation. It is a burden removed.

I am free to live once more.

Demons

Ghosts don't exist. They simply are not real. When a person dies, they cease to be—unless you're religious, then you have either heaven or hell. Dead people don't wander around on planet Earth, hiding out in rundown old farm houses. They just don't. My mother told me so a hundred times. So did my father.

Demons, well, they're a different thing altogether.

I saw it at the bottom of the list. My name, Jessa Leaner, big and bold in the late summer sunlight, showing I'd be one of the fortunate ones. I'd be sitting in Mrs. Corner's class for my fifth-grade year. That meant other kids, those less fortunate ones, would be forced to endure an entire school year under the rule of fat Miss Biddlewine. After all, Conklin Elementary School had just two fifth-grade classrooms. A kid's entire well-being depended upon the fate tossed at him or her by those in charge of assigning students to teachers.

Mrs. Corner, she'd been at it since my own parents had made their way through fifth grade, a kindly sort—not at all different from my own grandmother. Her classroom rested beneath a cozy atmosphere, with posters on the walls encouraging reading and writing and believing that anything and everything is possible for those who dared apply the effort. An aquarium at the rear of the room flashed the brilliant colors of exotic fish not native to our area—reds and blues and greens and yellows. Jiminy the gerbil worked furiously on the wheel inside a cage next to the fish tank—as if he, alone, powered the very lights overhead.

There weren't enough desks, though. Four neat rows of sixes added up to just twenty-four. Three of us didn't get there early enough to secure our places.

"There's room in Miss Biddlewine's class," Mrs. Corner explained, dismissing the overflow of kids standing at the back of the room.

Tommy Richter grinned at me from his seat, said, "Shit out of luck, Leaner. Off to the dungeon."

Three of us were forced to make the slow march down the hallway to the cold, bland, fishless, gerbil-less, poster-less confines belonging to the one nicknamed The Beast.

It didn't take long for me to wind up on the bad side of Miss Biddlewine. An A+ book report suffered with the markings of a D- after The Beast had become convinced that I hadn't fully read the assigned novel. But I *had* read it—the year before. So what if I forgot about the little twist at the end?

"You're a lying little cheat," she told me to my face.

"Am not," I argued.

Detention followed, a full week of missed recesses.

"I hate her," I told Shasta Cummings on the bus ride home from school that day.

Shasta said, "You do not."

We'd been best friends since before kindergarten, me and Shasta—even though we're complete opposites. Shasta, tall and blond and beautiful, scored all A's on her report cards and never spoke a bad word against anybody. Me? Short with brunette hair chopped in a pixie cut. And my grades, well, they were nearly as bad as my attitude—if you believed my mother.

"Okay," I relented, "maybe I don't *hate* her. Maybe I just don't like her very much."

The bus trundled down Grove Road past the old Fielding place. All eyes aboard the bus turned fearfully on the abandoned farmhouse. Nobody but squatters had bothered with the place since Elmer Fielding took a hammer and caved in the heads of his wife and three young children before shooting himself in the temple some thirty years earlier.

"We're going to stay the night in there on Halloween," Shasta boldly proclaimed.

Tommy Richter didn't believe a word of it. "Horse shit!" he spat. "Ain't nobody got guts enough to go in there at night. Even those squatters make sure they're out before sundown."

I had to side with Tommy on that one. Shasta had been saying we'd stay the night in the old Fielding place every Halloween since second grade. We never did, though.

Tommy's the one who brought it up. He said, "You know, Fieldings and Biddlewines are blood related." He shifted in his seat across the aisle from me and Shasta. "Rumor has it that Miss Biddlewine's mother was a Fielding."

"So what?" I retorted. "What's that got to do with the price of tea in China?"

"Means she might have it in her to just up and snap one day," Tommy explained, ambling toward the door to get off at his stop. "Crazy runs in families, I hear."

* * *

I didn't mean to say it out loud; it just sort of slipped past my lips and found its way into Miss Biddlewine's ears. Write an essay on what we hope to be when we grow up, she told the class.

Simple enough. I wanted to move to Hollywood and be an actress, I wrote. It's a dream I'd nurtured since the first time I ever saw *The Wizard of Oz* on TV. I yearned to be Dorothy, just wandering along my own yellow brick road. It didn't matter that I'd never acted in anything—I was simply too petrified to try out for the school plays year after year.

Miss Biddlewine's beady black gaze fixed on me like I'd brought a plague into her classroom. "You're joking, right?" she said. "A Hollywood actress? You? No, ma'am. An actress must be pretty and talented. You, Jessa Leaner, are neither. I suspect you'll amount to little more than a housewife to one of the local farmer boys. That will be *your* lot in life."

Anger got hold of me, convincing me that this was not the time to cry. Not in front of The Beast.

As I said, I didn't mean to say it out loud.

But the words fell out anyway.

Loud and hate-filled came my voice. "I hope you die!"

Gasps filled the room, sucking all the breathable air from my lungs. I wanted to apologize right there on the spot. But the thing about pride, well, pride is an obstacle.

Pride goeth before destruction.

Miss Biddlewine didn't react—at least not the way I figured she might. She simply dismissed me and called up the next student.

* * *

We all knew something bad had happened when we found Principal Goresline, rather than a substitute teacher, occupying Miss Biddlewine's desk.

"Died during the night," he said, his words fluttering above my head like evil accusing butterflies.

All those other kids looked on me as if I'd gone to Miss Biddlewine's house myself and did away with her.

The accusation from my conscience found its mark. *My fault!*

"She was fat," said Shasta. "She had a heart attack. You can't blame yourself because she ate too much."

But I'd said those words. I'd said them aloud.

Spoken words can never be taken back.

* * *

"It's a Ouija board," Shasta announced, cradling the box like she would a newborn baby. "We'll use it to conjure up Miss Biddlewine when we stay in the Fielding place tonight."

"My parents won't let me be out all night," I argued, hoping to talk her out of such a foolish notion.

"They'll never even know. You're telling them we're staying at my house, and my parents will think I'm staying with you."

I needed to know. I needed to ask Miss Biddlewine if she blamed me for her death.

"Does that thing work?" I wondered aloud, nodding at the box.

Shasta's reply came adamant, certain. "Of course it works. My cousin Janet used it to talk to our grandmother last Halloween. She asked private questions and the board answered correctly. It had to be Grandma because nobody else could have known the answers."

We walked up on the Fielding place just as the sun dropped below the horizon, leaving the sky streaked through with purple. First-floor windows had long ago been busted out by teenagers using the place for a hangout. Graffiti on the walls told tales about *this* girl or *that* one who might do things I'd never heard of before. Spent cigarette butts and empty beer cans littered the creaky floor.

"We'll sleep upstairs," Shasta said. "It's not as dirty up there."

Water stains painted ghostly images on the ceiling where the elements breached the leaky roof. Half-burned logs clogged a small fireplace inside the bedroom we claimed.

"Can you build a fire?" Shasta asked.

I tossed up a shrug, said, "Maybe we shouldn't."

I'd long ago learned to hate that dismissive *tsk* sound Shasta often employed. She knew as well as I did that I'd give in.

"Fine," I huffed, "—but I ain't taking the blame if this place burns down."

* * *

Shadows came out against the orange glow. Teasing dark shapes danced in corners, mocking our false bravado.

"Do you suppose he killed somebody in *this* room?" Shasta wondered.

He did—one kid in each bedroom as they slept. The wife, she'd been found in the kitchen. Fielding killed her as she prepared breakfast for her family.

We sat Indian style, facing each other, in front of the fire. The Ouija laid claim to the space between us. Candy bars and soda pops kept us in comfort.

Simple questions were asked as a means to calibrate the spirits. The oracle moved to either yes or no, depending on the knowledge we'd sought.

Shasta took control once we were satisfied we'd connect with somebody.

She asked, "Can we speak to Miss Biddlewine?"

The oracle slid across the board. Yes.

"I didn't mean it," I whined, hoping Miss Biddlewine herself might be listening. *"Honest."*

Letters began to pile up beneath the oracle, spelling out words I didn't want to know. KILL came first. Then, DEMON. DEATH and BLOOD followed.

"This ain't Miss Biddlewine," Shasta assured me.

I flung an accusation at her. "You're the one moving that stupid thing, aren't you?"

"I swear I'm not," Shasta promised.

All that soda pop and a case of the nerves got to me. "I gotta pee," I told her, gaining my feet.

"Hafta go outside," Shasta said. "Somebody smashed the toilet."

"Come with?" I asked, hoping to hide the pleading in my voice.

But Shasta wouldn't budge. The comfort of her sleeping bag won out over friendship.

Under my breath, I said, "I hope they get you."

The stairs creaked beneath my feet. Darkness swallowed the main-floor rooms. Outside, thick black clouds blotted out the moonlight. The night air had gone to a damp chill.

In the back of my head I could hear my mother's voice. *Be quick about it!*

Just beyond the back door I popped the snap and pulled my jeans down. That's when I heard it—heard *them*. Those whispered voices mocking me from somewhere inside that old death house. Shadows moved through the kitchen like tall dark ghosts, vaguely human in shape. I counted two of them against the blackness.

"Come inside," a whispered voice seemed to say.

Long, twisted fingers gripped the door frame.

A face, gaunt and hollow, peered out at me, watching me through black pools of nothingness where the eyes were meant to be.

I have no recollection of yanking my pants up, just of running across a field of soy beans, stumbling blindly toward my house.

My mother opened the door, said, "I thought you were staying at Shasta's house."

"Decided not to," I replied, slipping words between puffs of breath.

"Shoulda called. I'd have sent Daddy to pick you up. A girl shouldn't be wandering around at night."

I could still see that face: the empty gaze, protruding cheek bones, and the way its tongue dangled between cracked lips. Had he been one of Fielding's victims? A son, maybe?

* * *

Shasta's parents came looking for her the following day.

I don't know why, but I told them everything. I told them about staying at the Fielding place, the Ouija board, seeing the demon in the window.

They found Shasta's body in the room we'd shared. She'd been abused in ways you'd expect to read about on graffiti-covered walls.

Squatters, the police claimed. Drug addicts, judging by all the needles found.

I knew better, though. I'd seen the culprits.

Demons.

Family Tradition

They were there among the familiar names in Daddy's obituary. They sat in positions of honor above my name and those of my younger sister and baby brother. Unfamiliar names, these ones: Julie, Anna, and David. Our last name had somehow become attached to these strangers, thus attaching them to us—to Daddy.

"How come they're listed as survivors?" I dared ask my mother. I'd sprawled across her bed and took to watching her paint her puffy, reddened eyes with that hideous blue stuff.

Mother sat stone-faced at her vanity table and eyed me in the mirror. She said, "Because your father had a life before I came along."

Curiosity gnawed at my insides. A child should never question her parents, I'd long been taught. But I just had to ask. "What kind of life?"

"Same as the one he had with us, Lizabeth, only with different people. Now go get ready for the funeral."

Supposing she's right and I'm understanding exactly what she means, that would make Julie and Anna and David my older sisters and brother. Part of me liked that idea, while the other part took on a notion akin to offense at this uninvited intrusion that shoved me further down the Handly family totem pole.

"But I'm the oldest," I assured my mother, thus reassuring myself.

Mother disagreed, said so as if it's a fact everybody else had long known. "You're not the oldest, Lizzie. Never were."

* * *

A closed casket is what they called the proceedings. Had to be that way—on account of the damage done by the truck. The way I figured, if I couldn't see Daddy, well, then it would always remain a possibility that just maybe he's not really in there. Sort of like the way some people are convinced Elvis isn't really dead—or neither is Jim Morrison.

"He was just mowing the lawn," my mother is telling Lydia Scott's mom. The tears have a way of drawing her voice tight. "Mowed it a hundred times, he did."

Then the truck came off the road and ran him over—the end. We can't ever have him back again because some stupid old man decided he wasn't too drunk to drive home.

I hovered at the oak box, hoping…

"I held you once," the boy said, leaning closer to me than I'd have given permission—had it been sought. "You were just a tiny baby, of course. But then you took to fussing and your mother snatched you away."

David Handly, he claimed as his name; *David Handly Jr*—because David Handly Sr lay in that box holding my daddy's remains.

He asked, "How old are you now, Lizabeth?"

"Ten," I said. And I could see it then—Daddy's eyes looking back at me through David's gaze. "Did you know him?—my dad, I mean."

"I didn't see much of him since he and my mom split up." That big hand of his found my shoulder, gave it a gentle squeeze. "It's a hard thing, growing up without a father."

It's a lesson I would become familiar with in the coming years.

A line of people came through the funeral home, some I knew, others I'd never met.

David whispered, "Let's take us a ride."

"I have to ask my mother," I said, knowing full well she'd say no. She's just that way—half-brother or not, a boy should never be trusted.

I didn't bother with permission, though. She'd never ground me on the day we buried Daddy.

David's car—a dented white mess small enough to fit in a tall man's pocket—crouched in the far corner of the lot, eyeing us with suspicion as we approached. Inside grew a tangle of fast-food wrappers and empty Styrofoam coffee cups—just like Daddy's car.

David held the door for me, helped me into the passenger seat. "Daddy let me drive," I said, watching him slide behind the wheel. "I drove a hundred times."

He yanked at a pair of wires beneath the dash, twisted them together, set the engine in motion.

"How come you start it like that?" I asked.

Daddy's grin found his lips. "Lost my keys, is all," he explained. We didn't talk much during the ride; we just let the breeze passing through the windows do its dance between us. A rock and roll song played on the radio, though neither of us tapped our feet or hummed the melody.

"How about a Coke?" he asked, sliding the little white car into the empty lot across the street from the store he meant to visit.

"Why don't we park over there?" I wondered aloud, pointing at the Kwik-Stop Party Store. "I'll go in with you."

"I have to keep the car running—don't want anybody stealing it, do we?"

Traffic on Riley Road slowed him up, but David made it to the other side. He didn't bother with a stop at the cooler; Coca-Cola really didn't play a part in our trip. The pistol in his hand could have been a toy—the boy behind the counter knew better than me, though.

I took the driver's seat, slid the shifter to D, and parted traffic like Moses did the Red Sea.

"What are you doing?" David hollered, diving through the passenger window.

"Trying to get us out of here," I yelled. "Why'd you rob that place?"

All he could say was, "Jobs are for shmucks."

Same thing Daddy used to say.

Side streets kept us out of sight. David's head swiveled atop his neck, searched for those that could make life difficult.

"Slow down," he argued. "Don't draw attention."

We left the car two blocks from the funeral home. It never did belong to David.

"Sorry I dragged you along," he said, meaning to apologize.

"Nothing to be sorry about," I assured him. "I used to do the same thing for Daddy."

Quizzical—that's the sort of look he sported. "Drove getaway?"

I didn't answer. Some things are best left unspoken.

The Nick of Time

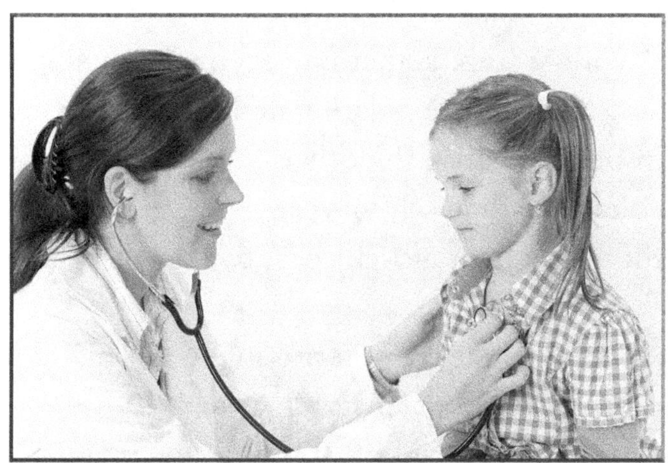

Its roots stretch back to the spring of 1968, a full year before the first man set his footprint on the moon, showing the world that anything is possible if we just reach for it. Optimism ran upright and strong that year. The world witnessed changes never seen before, and America took the lead on most of those endeavors.

Bethany Roberson couldn't quite grasp the enormity of the potential being mined across the planet. Those changes meant little to an 8-year-old beginning life in the quiet town of Williamston, Michigan. The fourth of five children—and the only girl—Bethany adapted to the rough play of her brothers, dishing out as many lumps as she received, toughening the girl in the eyes of neighborhood boys who'd long grown weary of entanglements that might put them on the losing end of a pretty solid left jab.

Scraped knees and split lips never bothered her. A broken right arm proved incapable of drawing tears from the girl. But that spring, back in 1968, the year the Detroit Tigers won the World Series, something seemed to fail inside her. Exhaustion crept in like a dark pall, bringing her low, keeping her in bed well after the other children had traipsed off to finish out the fading school year. The weight loss spooked her mother. Frequent nosebleeds twisted her father with worry.

Dr. Brandise spoke those terrifying words aloud to Bethany's parents: *Acute Lymphoblastic Leukemia.*

"There's nothing I can do for her," he confessed. "This one doesn't get better."

A few hospitals around the country might help stretch her time by a year or so, he offered—though that wasn't a guarantee. Nothing really ever is for certain in those sorts of matters.

Acute Lymphoblastic Leukemia is a blood disease, making it a nasty enemy that invades the whole body, leaving destruction in its wake. Those in the know call it The Wasting Disease. Nobody survives this war.

But Dr. Brandise, well, he reached into his pocket and sprinkled a few bread crumbs across the path the Roberson family had been forced upon.

"Memphis," he explained. "There's a children's hospital down there."

Words and phrases like *new drugs* and *experimental* fluttered in on gossamer wings of hope. But even hope doesn't arrive with promised fulfillment.

Second thoughts didn't figure into this equation. Desperation fueled determination, and so early in April, Mr. Roberson loaded his only daughter into the back of the family's Oldsmobile Vista Cruiser, and drove all night to a city known more for the blues and bar-b-que than for healing and miracles.

* * *

It came into existence six years earlier, back in 1962. Danny Thomas put the pieces into place, saying that "no child should die in the dawn of life." Father surely knows best. They called the place St. Jude Children's Research Hospital, naming it after the patron saint of hopeless causes.

They were bold in their intentions, proclaiming they would "cure" childhood leukemia one day. And true to their promise, significant successes have been gained behind a mysterious curtain few were allowed to pierce.

Doctors gathered in Bethany's room at the hospital, surrounding the girl as if she were a movie star. Blood was taken, workups performed, assessments made. Terms and phrases were scattered like seeds inside that tiny room. Hope sprouted here and there, growing, expecting to find harvest at the appropriate time.

They spoke in hushed tones about something called the *Total Therapy V Study*.

The medicines had come a long way in the few short years since the hospital came into being. But that didn't make it easier on the patients.

Liquid fire entered Bethany's body through an ever-present IV, burning her from the inside, leaving her too sick to keep a meal down. Sores opened on her hands. Muscles ached as if she'd aged by half a century.

"It's going to make you all better," her father promised.

Spinal taps introduced the girl to a most vivid sort of pain. Experimentation, it seemed. Throw it up and see what falls back down. A mixture of measured pharmaceuticals left her confused, light-headed, uncertain of all those promises on which she'd leaned.

She believed her father, though. He would see her through.

That's what daddies do.

Days bled into weeks. Hope ran wild like an escaped thoroughbred, appearing momentarily on any given day, only to be spooked back into the tangled brush, obscured and seemingly lost. But even so, gloom and doom didn't paint the whole affair black. Clowns visited the children in ward, bending balloons into poodles and monkeys and silly hats that made Bethany giggle for the first time since leaving home. Strawberry ice cream put things right—if only for an afternoon.

The fact that Bethany's hair had been coming out hadn't bothered the girl all that much. Mirrors weren't allowed on the floor. A visit from her mother and brothers in early May changed all that. The boys didn't mean to shake her. They'd just expected to find their sister as they last saw her—as they always knew her. The youngest cried and pulled away from her hug.

"He's just scared, is all," her mother explained. "He's still a baby."

Words couldn't soothe the girl's soul. "He's scared of *me!*" Bethany cried.

* * *

Needles and blood-letting became a matter of routine as summer followed its course. The darkness began giving way to more and prolonged moments of light. Their experiments were proving useful, fruitful, more than simply promising.

By late August, Bethany's leukemia had gone into remission.

"We won't use the word *cured* just yet," the doctors all said. False hope can really damage instinct and will.

With caution Bethany returned home at the start of fourth grade. Wigs covered her bald head. Home-cooked meals added to her weight. Even her brothers yanked her into their rough play in the family's backyard. But her friends, they stopped coming around, unsure if they might catch whatever had taken her from their midst.

Remission remained the good word that following July, when she visited St. Jude, on the very same day Neil Armstrong stepped onto the moon.

Her hair had returned—as did her friends—when Nixon traipsed off to China in 1972.

All those fears of relapse had vanished by the time Bethany Roberson graduated from high school in the spring of 1978.

College, marriage, children . . . all achieved—despite that original prognosis. She outlived both of her parents and her oldest brother, witnessed the births of four grandchildren, and celebrated thirty years of marriage. But even today, caution remains rooted within. It's become second nature to those who survive death sentences.

Dr. Brandise once called her a lucky girl for contracting leukemia in 1968. "A year earlier," he explained, "and you wouldn't have survived."

Timing is everything in life. Longevity is something that isn't guaranteed. It must be cultivated and worked on. It's to be wanted—despite the struggle. And most importantly, it must be earned.

Life and longevity is never a given.

Overcome (Holy Water)

The summer of 1965 brought me full-on into the beginnings of my teenage years. I'd reached my thirteenth birthday that June, and to hear grown folks tell about it, I'd become a man—or near about to being one. I didn't feel any different, though. I mean, I still liked to ride my bike and collect frogs along the riverbank.

I began to notice girls, too.

But that's another story for another time.

This one, the one I aim to tell here, is a story about water. By that I mean a story of life. See, water brings life to even desolate deserts. If water existed on the moon, there'd surly be some form of living creatures upon that lunar surface—microscopic, most likely.

We drink water to stay alive. Water gives life to the vegetables we plant in our fields. Rivers carve out shipping lanes for commerce. Those same rivers will run hydro-electric generators giving electricity to large metropolitan cities like Nashville, Birmingham, and Little Rock.

But water, well, it possesses other properties most folks won't even consider. Water changes people and places. It alters the living.

I came up in Little Rock, Arkansas, during those Jim Crow days. Being black meant I couldn't just waltz into the diner, slide into a booth, and order a hamburger, French fries, and a milk shake. It meant I had to search out the appropriate drinking fountain on those sweltering summer afternoons. It's just the way things were. Democrats had their say, and their say meant segregation of the races—even though my mama always said there ain't but one race: the human race.

Long about the time I reached my thirteenth year, things began to change. Oh, sure, there were those who resisted federal orders seeking to desegregate the South. Men like Governor George Wallace of Alabama or our own Orval Faubus here in Arkansas spoke openly of *segregation forever.* But it was all those smaller voices along the Arkansas River that carried the heaviest of words.

"Know your place, boy," rang a common refrain from the likes of Jimbo Rutherford. Rutherford, and men like him, went to great lengths to hold on to the old ways.

"Know your place, boy."

"Just don't sass back," my mother told me each time I left our house.

Rutherford, though, he'd search me out, approach me like I'd stole from him—even if I was in my own dang yard.

"Know your place, boy."

I hated that man. I hated him in my very heart—even though Jesus tells us to do otherwise. Inside my head I'd devise ways of killing him with the most painful of notions.

I even tried being nice to him once, back when I was eight or nine years old. "Afternoon, sir," I'd said, walking past his house on the river.

"Know your place, boy," is all he gave back.

My mother claimed he was just bitter because he owned as much as colored folks and nothing else. I guess he figured he deserved more, and I'm the one that stood in his way.

Jimbo Rutherford was a large man. Even other white folks would think twice before engaging with him in simple conversations. Jimbo's love of Kentucky Bourbon added to the tainted picture most folks painted of the man.

Now, I know what you're wondering. What's this got to do with water? I'll get to that in due time.

* * *

Bedford is the name my father gave me at birth. It followed in line back to his grandad. Bedford Samuel Rawlings IV. My mother claimed it had a ring of nobility about it. I just hated being called Fordy.

I tried for a nickname of my own making once. I began telling friends to call me Samson, like the strong man in the

Bible. I even lied to folks, told them that's my middle name. My father found out and set folks straight.

"His name ain't no *Samson*," he'd hollered. "He's to be called Bedford or Fordy."

I almost hated him for that one.

I didn't, though.

Hate my own daddy?

Nope.

So, long about the time I'd turned thirteen, we'd gone through a long dry stretch where most were wondering if we'd ever see rain that summer. Most blacks, they were still sharecropping back then. A failed crop would mean disaster for families all over Arkansas.

Water! Can't grow what's been planted without it.

My family was no exception. Everything we owned came from the hard work done in the fields. While we didn't live on the farm, most of my days were spent there, picking tomatoes, cucumbers, or cotton—depending on where help was needed. Without that precious rain, there'd be nothing to pick, nothing to sell, nothing to eat.

Hand to mouth, my daddy called that sort of existence.

Now, where we lived, the roof over our heads was little more than a shotgun shack, situated along the banks of the Arkansas River. Living on the river allowed for certain benefits. We'd not go hungry, what with the abundance of fish to be had in those flowing waters. But catfish won't pay rent to the white man who owns that shack I just mentioned.

Mama took in laundry from the better-off black families in the area. Daddy wouldn't budge off his prohibition against her washing white folks' clothes, though. He saw it as a sort of handout—taking anything from the *man*.

"We gonna be just fine on our own," he'd argue whenever Mama broached the subject.

Her eyes would fix on him while her finger pointed at me, saying, "That boy gonna need new trousers before too long."

Daddy would just shrug it off, saying he'd find a means.

And he usually did.

* * *

"Gonna have rain today?" It's the common question heard most that year.

The days would end without a single drop from God.

Fields had gone to dust long about the middle of July. Even the river had taken to running slower than usual. Those that owned the fields took a look at hauling water from the river to irrigate those seeds sitting in the dirt.

"A thing like that might work," my daddy said at a meeting on Billy Daniels's property.

"Know your place, boy," Jimbo Rutherford argued, eyeing him with disdain.

Billy Daniels spoke in Daddy's defense, said, "We gonna need every pair of hands to get this done, Jimbo, no matter they be white or black. It's the only way to save what's left of the growing season."

Jimbo sneered at the man, but offered nothing by way of response.

* * *

By the first of August, seedlings began to sprout in fields across the county. The river-water idea showed great promise. But that wouldn't be near enough to bring in a normal haul.

And then it happened.

First, Dr. King paid a visit to Little Rock, giving a fiery speech on civil rights to a crowd of the city's black folks. Afterwards, he laid it all out there in prayer to the Almighty.

A week later, the heavens opened up, dropped water all across the state.

Thankful at first, souls began to worry when the deluge refused to know its place.

The banks washed out along the river. Those folks that lived closest ran to the higher grounds, supposing it wouldn't reach that far beyond. Thing is, a river won't pay any mind to boundaries and lines drawn in sand. It goes where it will.

Men with shovels formed lines to resist, filling sand bags and building walls.

"Ain't gonna hold," my daddy said.

It didn't. Water wandered over sand bags, on up the slope leading toward those shacks put up during the Great Depression. White and black alike watched their homes wash away into the muddy Arkansas.

I recall my father talking to Hubert Sumner about where the river might crest. Elders who'd been on those banks for generations swore it wouldn't get much higher. Floods never went past the Cordon property—which was below our place.

Sunset brought a different version of this story.

Water began lapping at the front steps of our porch. The threat stood strong. Shovels went abandoned, men grabbed their wives and children, and made for the city.

There comes a time when home just isn't there where you remember it to be. The floor of our place went dark with the river's reaching embrace. Furniture, the things my daddy scraped and saved for, found a current and took leave.

"Dear Jesus," my mother prayed. In the matter of a few hours she'd been changed, aged a dozen years that wouldn't be lived out.

Water will do that.

Mr. Charlie, our neighbor, waded up to our front door, said, "It's time to move out, folks."

Stubbornness had long been my father's worst trait—according to my mother. That day, the one that changed everything, my daddy conceded.

* * *

Skiffs and rafts moved with the river's flow, taking weary souls away from all they'd known. My father helped my mother onto Mr. Charlie's makeshift raft, then pulled himself up. His hand reached for mine.

"Come on, Son," he said, touching the tips of my fingers.

I got scared, though. Dark water churned at my chin, steps and slopes hidden beneath tricked my balance. Under the surface, the rush grew angry.

"*Daddy!*" I cried, losing footing against the river's rage.

"Boy can't swim," I heard him say, directing Mr. Charlie in my direction.

I called for him again. That's when the water had its say, filled my mouth with its filth, polluted my lungs, yanked me under without a passing thought.

I'd been baptized in this water only a year prior.

"Holy water," my mother called it. "Gonna wash your soul."

There's a fighting at first, when a person is drowning. It's just natural instinct, I suppose. But then comes that point where even the body knows enough to let go the struggle.

I can't say I saw the white light others have mentioned. I did catch hold on that peace, though—even as the river pulled me to its bottom and moved me along its wending ways. I recall voices there, underwater, talking *about* me rather than *to* me. Too many voices to make out the words they were using.

Notions of rescue fled like crooks from the law. The Arkansas River would be my grave.

Funny how plans get shifted and rearranged to resemble a thing we'd never contemplated as an outcome. That hand grabbed hold on my shirt and yanked me up with the very force of God Himself.

"Come on, Son!" a panicked voice hollered. *"Breathe, dammit!"*

I heard the ruckus from somewhere above—me being the one overhead. I didn't see the commotion—at least not with my eyes. I just came to appreciate the effort going into bringing me back.

"Don't you die, Son!"

I tried for words of my own, but nothing made it to sound.

Hands, big and powerful, pressed against my chest, urged that holy water from my lungs.

Choked, I did, on that filthy river water. Coughed it up all over the floor of that wooden skiff.

"Daddy!" I cried out.

But the one who saved me wasn't my father.

"You're gonna be just fine, Son," Jimbo Rutherford assured me.

I guess you might call it fear, that big-eyed gawk I tossed on him. *What happens next?* I wondered. *Will he throw me overboard?*

He did no such thing, though.

He's the one who pulled me back among the living.

"You're gonna be just fine, Son," he repeated, as if I was some sort of kin to him.

My folks were waiting to claim me up high, where the water left off. My father had that look like I'd been snatched by the Klan.

My mother knew better. She understood just fine.

"Water changes everything," she said, once I'd come ashore.

* * *

That Jimbo Rutherford saved my life would never be spoken of aloud. My father chose to see it as a thing I did for myself. My mother, well, she gave credit to the hand of God. Even Jimbo would take that knowledge to the grave, never making mention of that night.

Of course, he never called me boy again. Never told me to know my place, either.

As I grew older, I came to understand it just fine.

Water really does change everything.

Saint Thomas

It began with a fever—a hundred five spike—right after the injections. He rode that for two whole days before it finally broke. When the fever left, it washed away his budding personality, that spark which had only just begun to gain form and shape. It's who he'd been meant to be, that early glimpse now gone. They claimed the injections had nothing at all to do with his current condition.

A mother knows better.

He hides in the closet most days, right after the other kids get home from school. He doesn't hide because he's scared of them. Thomas hasn't a grasp on the concept of fear. He hides to avoid playing requests.

"I just wanna play my songs," he says each day he enters the closet, "not theirs."

His songs, the ones he composes while the other kids are away for the day. Thomas doesn't like an audience. The other kids, though, they all want to hear him play pop songs on his piano.

"Play Rihanna," Paige always says.

"No," Billy will argue, "play that one song—the one from that movie."

If caught outside the closet, Thomas will oblige the younger sibling requests—but only grudgingly. He has an ear for song. One listen and he has it down note for note. It's all part of the spectrum his doctors are always going on about.

Autism made my son a musical genius. At least that's what his pediatrician claimed, way back when Thomas turned five and first climbed a piano bench. Beethoven dripped from his tiny fingers as if he'd been playing for a lifetime.

Reincarnation, my husband claimed. "He's one of the greats come back to life."

It's never as simple as that. Quirks accompany his talent. Thomas couldn't go to school with the neighbor kids. He didn't have it in him to connect, to engage with other human beings outside of family. Home schooling gave him incredible grades, though college proved one of those abstract dreams we never really managed to bring to fruition.

"Suppose you just play that Rihanna song once?" I ask, bartering his talent to appease my daughter. "Paige will leave you alone if you play it once."

There's no answer from the closet. He's inside his head again.

"Quit being such a baby, Tommy," Billy argues. "Just play that song we heard yesterday—the one from that cop show."

Billy and Paige are still amazed at Thomas's one-listen knack. So are his doctors—and a host of others who see concert revenue or music-download sales rather than a young man dealing with mental deficiencies.

We never treated Thomas differently from the two younger kids. And believe me when I say the boy has always been different.

"I'll play one of my own songs," he says from inside the closet. "I made a new one today."

But Billy and Paige aren't impressed with songs they've never heard before.

Billy whines, "How are we supposed to know if you're even playing it right?"

Paige stomps her foot, says, "You're so selfish, Tommy." She doesn't mean it, though; she corrects herself the way she does so often with her oldest brother. "No you're not, Tommy. You're not selfish. I'm sorry I said that to you."

Paige is my youngest. She's just eight years old, but her soul is as old and wise as the Dalai Lama's. She used to believe Thomas had abilities beyond the music. She'd tell him things from her heart—sort of like whispered prayers. And Thomas, he'd just tell her, "Okay. I'll do it."

"Make the kitty cat come back home." And then our long-missing cat appeared at the front door.

"Make Grandpa not have cancer anymore." Then some doctor pronounced my father cancer-free.

"Make me autistic," she asked, "so I'll be just like you."

That's the only time Thomas ever refused her prayer.

Of course it's never really Thomas performing these miracles.

I wanted so much more for this firstborn—the way any mother wants for her child: A girl he'd love forever, his own children to dote over, the prestige of some amazing career that would have me telling the neighbors just how brilliant my boy has always been. But girls scare him. And they scare me, as well. They'll only damage him further. I've seen those anxious moments where interaction threatens to ignite the air, leaving all involved scarred and lost.

It never breaks out that way, though. It's just easier to extract the boy from the potential.

I never blamed God. God's not the one who brought the child to the pediatrician. But we'd learned from the firstborn what not to do with those who would follow. Paige and Billy have never felt the prick of a needle.

"Mine first," Thomas says, stepping from his place of hiding. "Then I'll play their songs."

Paige takes his hand and leads her big brother to his place of honor. "I love you, Tommy," she says, leaving tiny kisses on his knuckles.

Thomas loves her, too—he just lacks that sort of emotional vocabulary to allow for a verbal response.

At that piano, he's right where he's meant to be. Long fingers hover over the keys for a hushed moment before taking to dance, filling the house with delicate notes strung together like a strand of beautiful pearls. The mournful piece rises from the boy's heart, confesses the sadness in which he drowns.

I'm the one who cries at these moments. But I no longer weep for lost potential. These are tears of thanksgiving for what I have. Thomas is ours, the firstborn of three. The one I love most—though I'd never admit that out loud.

"I love you, Tommy," Paige says again, wrapping her arms around her sturdy idol.

"Okay," Thomas says, his stiff posture relenting, his body taking a lean into his baby sister. "I'll play Rihanna now."

Sweetie Girl

I don't know why I even bother. It's not like we were ever close. You failed me when Dad died. You failed me and Jeffrey. But Jeffrey's the smart one. He knew to get out before it fell apart, before we (you) lost our home, after we (you) squandered Dad's savings—Dad's, because you never worked a day in your life—and his meager life-insurance benefits.

"That's not cream, Mom," I tell you yet again, as you stir a tablespoon of margarine into your coffee.

You eye me with that curious suspicion you've mastered in recent months. "And who are you again?" you ask.

It's the disease, I remind myself. "I'm Carol Ann," I inform you, "your daughter."

"Oh!" That's your only response to something so personal, so deep, so truthful.

I hate you for this—even though it's not your fault.

Your pale blue eyes no longer shine. They fix on me with unspoken accusation. "I forget things," you say. "It wasn't always like this."

"I know, Mom. It's called Alzheimer's."

"And who decided that?"

"Your doctor."

You rise from your chair like you mean to let me have one across the face. "Now you listen to me, Miss Lillian Know-it-all, I'm—"

"I told you, I'm Carol Ann." I rise against you, ready to block the blows you've taken to throwing these last few weeks. "Aunt Lillian is dead, Mom."

It's there in your confusion, that brief moment of understanding, as if you're recalling that memory you scarcely spoke of before doctors pronounced you doomed.

"Of course," you say, settling back into your position of comfort. "I know you're not her. She's dead—been so for years."

"Ten," I say. "Ten years."

You draw a sip from your buttered coffee. "Now, who are you again?"

I don't answer you. Why should I? It'll only be lost to you the moment I speak.

It returns for a moment, that wisp of remembrance behind your gaze. "There was that boy," you say, scratching at the dust that has become your memory. "Who was that boy you were always with?—the one with the scar on his chin?"

"Jeffrey," I remind you. "He's your son, Mom."
"And whatever became of him?"

* * *

I'm the one doing the dishes these days. You aren't capable of even that much anymore. I'm also in charge of the laundry and the cooking and bathing you.

Did you resent me and Jeffrey when we were too young to do these things for ourselves?

Jeopardy blares from the television. It's still your favorite show. Only now, instead of impressing others with the correct answer to some obscure French literary question, you yell *ketchup* at the screen when Alex Trebek asks about the last man on the moon.

Jeffrey won't come to visit. You're already dead to him, because you no longer recognize him. He can't handle that. He can't take not being your favorite anymore.

Yes, favorite. I can say it now without the hurt normally attached to such a notion. Jeffrey and I always understood this fact. He's the golden boy, the college grad, Dr. Fantastic, the one that did something with his life. Me? I'm just you for a different generation. No college, a miserable marriage, a bored housewife with two kids that could care less if I died tomorrow.

Your voice rises in that irritated way it does when you think everybody is out to get you. "Lillian!" you holler. "I did *not* give you permission to change the television channel."

But it is *you* that has changed the television channel.

"You're sitting on the remote, Mother," I explain, reaching beneath you to retrieve the device. "And Lillian is still dead."

That's when I see it, that familiar light behind your blue eyes.

Recognition!

"Carol Ann." You say it with a hushed reverence, as if my name belonged to a favorite martyred saint. "You've come to see me."

The gentleness of your fingers brushing the tear from my cheek stirs recollections of a summer day in 1969, when I'd crashed my bike and, for that afternoon, I felt like your favorite, the way you nursed my scraped knee.

You ask, "Why are you crying, sweetie girl?" The timbre of your voice rings much younger than your seventy-five years.

"Sweetie girl," I say, repeating the nickname you haven't used for me in forty years. "You remember, Mom?"

"Of course I remember. You're my child, Carol Ann."

It's a moment that won't last, so I slip it in where I can. "I love you, Mom," I whisper, pressing a kiss to your forehead. "I hope you know that."

But then, just as quick as it comes, it goes. I'm Lillian again—Lillian, your dead sister.

And I resent you again.

Not you, really. I resent the diagnosis. I resent knowing I've lost you, that we'll never be close.

I resent knowing it could happen to me twenty years down the road.

"Lillian's dead, Mom," I say, returning to the kitchen. "Lillian's dead."

Wordless

"What's that word say?"

"That's an easy one, Daddy. Just sound it out."

Levi Bacchus can't read. 36 years old, and he'd never learned the meaning of a single sentence.

"I just ain't cut out for this, Jamie Lynn."

The girl's countenance dropped in disagreement—just like her mother, that one.

"So, you're a quitter now?" she bellowed, sounding too much like the woman who'd walked out of their lives two years earlier.

Levi took offense. "Mind your manners, Missy. I ain't never been called no quitter."

"Reading is something everybody should be able to do, is all I'm saying."

"It's easy for you," Levi argued. "You're just a kid, still in school. You have teachers telling you what to do and how to do it. I'm just too old for learning."

The girl narrowed her gaze, jabbed a finger into the open book. "From the beginning," she demanded.

His heaving huff meant he'd do it again—if only for her sake.

Words formed in his head before finding place on his tongue. Some came through in broken bits and pieces, while others arrived fully formed and ready for sound.

Jamie's excitement in the matter is why he kept trying. Well, that and the fact he'd long desired the ability to pick up the morning paper and offer complaint or praise for the direction of the nation. All those people in the break room at the plant held their own opinions on everything from the president to the latest championship season enjoyed by the local high school football team.

"That's good, Daddy," Jamie said, patting her father on the arm. "That's really good. You'll be reading books before too long."

A smile worked at the edges of his lips, refusing to go unnoticed.

"I'd like that, Sweet Pea." That's all he'd say of the matter. If it came to that, well then, he'd have accomplished something worth appreciating.

Levi harbored bigger notions than merely reading books. When a man can read, he can do or be anything he wants. His own father often said a man who can't read is forever in bondage. How can a man truly be free if he cannot read the document spelling out the very rights bestowed upon him by simple virtue of birth? No sir. Being illiterate no longer appealed to him.

Of his immediate family—father, mother, two older brothers—only Levi failed to attend college. Oh, he graduated from high school. Being a star quarterback will afford that sort of luxury. But when those coaches from the universities came calling, low test scores couldn't open doors that promised more than a life spent in auto factories.

He'd seen a show on TV about a man who'd been sent to prison for five years for armed robbery. While there, this man learned to read, took a course on the law, and became a legal secretary upon his release. Eight years later, he'd earned a law degree and opened his very own practice.

Levi didn't see himself arguing cases in a court of law—defending criminals most likely to be guilty just didn't appeal to his sense of right and wrong. What he did see, however, is the need for a good and honest person to run the city he'd forever called home.

"Think I could be mayor?" he asked his daughter.

Jamie Lynn always grinned over such talk. "Everybody has to have a dream, Daddy."

It's what she always says.

Everything begins with a dream.

She gets that part of her from her mother.

"Once I can read without stopping to ask questions," he mused, "maybe I'll throw my hat into the ring, huh?"

"There's nothing wrong with asking questions," she answered, weaving wisdom between her words.

* * *

She'd been a Girl Scout, his daughter—Daisies and Brownies before that. It's the other girls who bullied her out of the joy that sort of thing once offered. Straight A's have a way of making others feel inferior, even threatened.

But Jamie Lynn isn't the type to pine or fret. She chose to tutor—and not just her father, either. Kids come to the house needing to know this and that among mathematics or English or science. Her dream? To be a teacher one day.

And she'll accomplish that much and more.

Her mother had that very same sense about her, as well. She knew what she wanted in life and cleared the path upon which she traveled.

High school sweethearts, they'd been, Jamie Lynn's mother and father. She'd been the pretty cheerleader; he'd been the All-American boy with a cannon for an arm. She went to college, he didn't.

But she returned to him, joyfully accepting his proposal for a life together. Her degree carried her back to the high school from which they'd both graduated. This time, rather than student, she became teacher—American History.

Levi went to work building Cadillacs in the local plant. It paid well, offered medical benefits, and paid vacation time. Life settled into routines.

Then came their little bundle. This didn't sit well with the newly minted history teacher. No sir. It's as if Levi had intentionally sabotaged his own wife's career in some fiendish plot to keep her home.

Words of love became "stupid" and "ignorant" and "illiterate ass." She walked out one evening and never came back to the home they'd built together.

A former student, he'd heard—five years her junior. They'd run off together, supposedly making a new home somewhere out west.

Levi didn't challenge it. He received the house and the kid in exchange for his signature on those papers he couldn't even read.

Jamie Lynn, she's the light that shined in his darkness, showed him there's still so much more living to be done. And learning to read, well, that just added to the adventure.

* * *

The night came when he read an entire chapter from one of Jamie Lynn's old middle-school books—straight through, unpunctuated by all those starts and stops and nervous questions. By the end of the month, Levi had managed the entire story—all 207 pages.

"We have to celebrate, Daddy," she insisted.

It'd been the silly draw of embarrassment that twisted his head left and right, his voice saying, "No need to make a fuss, Sweet Pea."

But fuss is only the beginning. "Dinner and a movie," she ordered. "Then we'll stop off at the mall and pick out a few books that you might like."

There were stories he recalled from his boyhood, books other kids clutched under their arms and took for granted. Stories that stirred so much excitement in those young lives.

They'd belong to him now.

"You're finally blooming, Daddy—just like a flower."

And so was his daughter.

A teacher in the making.

Memory of a Robot (An Essay)

It's usually a song or a taste or a smell that draws out long-dormant memories tucked inside the mind, buried beneath mundane daily clutter, like a favorite summer shirt packed away for winter, awaiting the spring thaw and a new beginning.

Some memories are retrieved more often than others. The smell of pine needles and the dulcet tones of Nat King Cole singing "Chestnuts Roasting on an Open Fire" trigger remembrance of Christmas past, sparking discussion of knitted sweaters Grandma fashioned each year for the grandkids. Or the time Santa brought older brother Billy a new dirt bike, ushering in the turmoil of jealousy between siblings.

Maybe one taste of Rocky Road ice cream is enough to conjure mental images of first love—found one afternoon while vacationing in Florida during sixth-grade spring break.

The smell of fresh-cut grass does it for me. There is a virtual Rolodex of memories attached to that one scent. It's one of the earliest mental triggers I can recall. It's strongest in late spring or early summer, when snow and cold are discarded for sunshine and warmth, and that first mowing of the season is underway.

I remember one such day, back when I was just five years old. One of the neighbors had gotten to his lawn first, stirring up that fragrant smell that made good on the promise of no more snow—at least for several long months.

My father, determined not to fall further down the totem pole of neighborhood lawn care, rushed out to the shed in our backyard. Now, this wasn't one of those cheap little metal sheds that are known to blow away with only the slightest provocation. No sir. This one was made of wood and paint and windows with real glass panes. Inside, a small stove offered heat during the cold months. A large workbench occupied most of the rear wall.

The lawnmower brooded in the corner, incensed over being ignored since the previous October.

"It's going to need gas," my father said, stepping over the various collectables that had gathered there in the shed during the winter. "But first we'll to have to clean up this place so I can move around in here. Who wants to help?"

As I mentioned earlier, I'd been just five that year. My sister and older brother were seven and eight. We'd yet to become teenagers that preferred the comfort in slinking off and shirking anything resembling responsibility.

"We'll help!" came our shouts.

Stuff began to be moved here and there. Those items we'd keep were set aside for reassignment. The rest of the mess found refuge in a trash pile, destined for discarding come garbage pickup day.

"We'll keep these coffee cans," my dad said. "Those will be perfect for storing nuts and bolts, nails and screws."

But there were more than were needed.

A *lot* more.

A grin attached itself to my father's expression. "I've got an idea."

Dad's ideas had a way of turning a dull afternoon into something we kids would remember long after that day.

Coffee cans sat piled upon the workbench. Dad's welder sparked into action. After a short period, those cans were joined together in long tubular forms.

"These will be the legs," Dad explained.

Legs?

Holy cow!

Doctor Frankenstein had nothing on my father.

Smaller cans became the arms of whatever creation my dad saw inside his mind.

An old vacuum cleaner figured prominently into the torso of this incredible new being.

A trash can, old hubcaps, perhaps an expired license plate or two—these all went into the glorious monster my dad determined would see life before the end of the day.

Finally, after an entire afternoon of puttering, my father unveiled his masterpiece, right there in our backyard, where half a dozen neighbor kids had congregated, hoping to see a thing they'd never be able to forget.

It stood eight feet tall—at least to a five-year-old boy!

Coffee can legs stood sturdy and ready for battle—should Uncle Sam require its use in Vietnam.

"What's that plug for?" somebody dared ask.

Dad's grin grew wider than I'd ever recalled seeing before.

A heavy orange extension cord traveled the distance from the shed to the very spot where that beast awaited the jolt of electricity that would zap life into its metal body.

Dad plugged it in; his fingers found the switch on the vacuum cleaner torso.

Click!

The Mighty Heap vibrated, whirred, growled, and shook.

And that's all it did. Nothing more, nothing less. It didn't delight us by marching through the streets. It didn't open its mouth and utter some profound thing.

It simply stood its ground and sounded just like, well, a vacuum cleaner.

Laughs were issued, pictures were snapped—though I'm not sure where those photos are today. Doesn't matter. I can still recall most of the details of this robot's short-lived life.

It's tucked away inside my head, easily replayed whenever that first mowing of the spring takes place.

All those other kids, the ones who dropped by that day to bear witness, they probably don't remember that afternoon in 1972. Dad's robot may not have made much of an impression—at least not the way it did on me.

My father is no longer here. So, it's these little moments—silly as they were—that keep him very much alive to me. These are moments before alcohol became his weakness, changing him from that fun dad into somebody who at times was a stranger. One day I'll be gone, as will my siblings, and there won't be anybody left to recall that day Mr. Weeks built his coffee can/vacuum cleaner monster in the backyard of our family home.

I'll hold on to my memories for as long as I'm able, breathing in those triggering smells, cranking up familiar songs, or smiling over some faded old photograph capturing another one of those simple moments. Our memories will be lost one day, and the following generations will gaze upon our tattered pictures and ask, "Who were these people, and what were they doing?"

But don't fret. A new summer is upon us. There's grass to mow and memories to make. How we determine to save those moments is entirely up to us.

Monster

"Indecent liberties with a minor," my mother explained, repeating the same words Danny Deagle sprinkled on us kids earlier in the day. "I don't want you girls trick-or-treating at his house tonight."

The old man at the end of the street, she meant. A swirl of new words followed him into our neighborhood—words shrouded in secrecy, in a thick fog of mystery. The simple ones I'd commit to memory, intending to find them in the dictionary I got for my tenth birthday this past summer—a secret gift that nobody else knew about.

Perv—that's the one I looked up last night, right before bed. Millicent, my older sister, she used it when telling Grandma Myron about the new neighbor in question. But if there's such a word as perv, well, old Merriam-Webster hasn't been told. I couldn't find it to save my life.

"I ain't going anywhere near that side of the street," Millicent announced. "—not as long as he's lurking down there."

She'd go over there, though. Millicent thinks she's hot you-know-what just because she's thirteen now. Besides, every kid in the neighborhood wants to be the first one to walk up those front steps and ring the doorbell. You have to be seen doing it, though, or it won't count for anything.

I tossed in a handful of words meant to be my two cents. "Danny Deagle says he got in trouble down in Kentucky before he got in trouble here in Ohio—that old man, I mean."

Danny Deagle knows about these sorts of things. His stepdad is a cop.

My mother lit a fresh Marlboro and proclaimed, "He's got no business staying on this street—not with all you kids around." Thin lazy smoke slithered from her nostrils like twin snakes in search of a meal. "Don't let me hear that you girls went trick-or-treating at his house."

* * *

Millicent dressed as a belly dancer again—same as last Halloween and the one before that. She just likes the attention from boys like Danny Deagle and Jeff Brahm. But they like her only because she's practically naked in her costume.

Me? I got stuck being a hobo again—even though my mother promised me I could be the belly dancer this year.

Millicent grabbed her pillowcase from the kitchen table and said, "Ready, dweeb?"

"You're the dweeb," I argued, snatching my own pillowcase.

My mother said, "Don't stay out all night."

We'd stay out as long as it took to fill those pillowcases to the full.

Danny Deagle met us in front of his house. Those gray eyes of his drank up Millicent like she's cool water and he's been thirsty for days. But he really couldn't be blamed. Booty shorts and a sports bra, that's all she wore underneath that sheer white fabric that left her belly bare and exposed.

Our father, before he remarried and moved to Cincinnati, wouldn't have allowed one of his daughters to go traipsing through the neighborhood wearing only a couple of tissue papers.

But our father doesn't come around anymore. And our mother, she won't play the villain—as she likes to say. So Millicent gets away with murder.

Kids of all ages crisscrossed our neighborhood exchanging tricks for treats. Smarties and SweetTarts mingled with fun-sized Snickers and Milky Ways in the bottom of our pillowcases. And later, when we'd finally have to call it a night, Millicent would try to swindle me out of all of my Hershey's Miniatures, offering junk like jelly beans and peanut butter chews for trade.

Billy Pinsler found us where Delbert Avenue and McCaully Drive cross. Billy's my age—only shorter. "Anybody going to the perv's house?" he asked.

Danny fixed me in his sight. “You’ll go up there, won’t you, Melanie?”

My head twisted left and right. “Mom said to stay away from his house,” I told him, knowing full well he’d poke and prod until I agreed to answer his dare.

Danny’s good like that. He knows how to get kids to do what he’s too scared to do—only he’d never admit to being scared.

Millicent joined the push, said, “Since when do you listen to Mom?”

We were already there, bags half-full, in front of that house on the end of our street. I’d be the one going, as usual.

“Melanie won’t go,” Billy announced. “She’s too scared.”

My eyes found Millicent’s eyes. “You’re the one who’s half naked; why don’t you go up there?”

“Because the guy’s a perv, nimrod!” said Danny. “You want him to try something with her?”

And what about me?

I tossed my gaze toward that house. A lone porch light shined out of the dark.

“If I scream,” I said, walking to my demise, “you better run and call the cops.”

A fall breeze passed through the trees overhead, sending loose leaves gliding to the ground.

My legs went heavy and stiff, unwilling to move without provocation. Somewhere on that street a dog barked warnings at kids in costumes.

My body halted at the bottom step leading to the front door. I tossed a glance over my shoulder. Millicent, Danny, and Billy took refuge behind shrubs at the foot of the driveway.

"Ain't gotta be scared," the voice said, suddenly there like a spook in the night. "Just come on up. I won't bite—except you want I should."

A bead of sweat raced down my belly, which was stuffed with an old pillow to make me look fat.

Gray hair going thin twisted this way and that, like weeds, atop his head. Skinny, like maybe he'd been sick for a while.

My foot found the first step, brought us closer.

He asked, "You gonna say it?"

I would. It only seemed right. "Trick or treat."

A laugh just like my father's laugh slipped past his lips. He kind of resembled him, too, around the eyes and nose.

"You say it with no real conviction, girl," he said, almost accusing me of something.

The mouth of my pillowcase yawned wide, ready to swallow whatever treats he chose to dispense.

Two Hershey's miniatures.

Mr. Goodbar and Krackle.

"Where's your sister?" he wondered aloud, throwing his gaze like a pair of marbles down the driveway.

"Hiding," I confessed, backing away.

But those eyes of his—cobalt blue, same as my father's—took hold on me, wandered along my length as if sizing me for a new dress.

“You s’posed to be a bum?” he asked.

Denim coveralls, a gray t-shirt that used to be white, and worn-out tennis shoes seemed the easiest of Halloween costumes to put together.

I corrected him, said, “A hobo.”

“Hobo, huh?” He waggled his finger, drew me closer to his grasp. “Take the rest of these,” he said, offering me the entire bowl of miniatures.

“What about the other kids?”

“Ain’t no other kids. You the only one come ’round tonight.”

It made my bag heavier and more than satisfied, this extra loot.

My voice came tight, higher-pitched than normal. “Thank you.”

“Polite—just like your daddy at that age.” The weight of his body found relief against the door frame. “Did you get the *Merriam-Webster* I sent for your birthday?”

My head tipped a nod, my voice said, “Thank you, Granddad.”

* * *

“Did he lose his goo over you?” Danny Deagle asked, acting like a big brother. “I’ll tell my stepdad if he did.”

“He didn’t,” I assured him, not really understanding what goo just might get lost.

Millicent’s gaze took hold on mine, passed words into my head, words demanding my silence on the matter.

Aloud, her words asked, "What'd he give you?"

"Jellybeans," I told her. "Nothing but jellybeans.

It's Only Sex

She's says it's only sex—as if that settles the matter and he has no say whatsoever. But he should have a say because she's his and he's hers and that's just the way it's supposed to be.

He says, "We don't need the money that bad, Melissa."

She replies, "We do so—unless you don't mind sleeping in a car we can't afford to keep gassed up." She finds him leaning against the frame of the bathroom door, watching her, watching the whole routine of preparing for a date that doesn't include him. "I love you, Tommy. You have to know that."

"Then why—"

"We've been through this a dozen times just this morning alone." It's that sharpness in her voice that gives away her mood, paints the girl argumentative, unbending. "You're the one who quit your job, not me!"

Tommy tosses out the same retort he's used since the moment she suggested this foolish idea. "Why can't you just ask your folks for a loan?"

To ask for help means defeat. It tells her parents she can't make it on her own.

It proves them correct in their opinion of him.

Melissa finds his gaze in the mirror. "I'm not going to listen to them call you worthless, Tommy."

Her sisters went to college—all three of them. Melissa didn't even finish high school. And that's Tommy's fault because if she hadn't been in love with him, well, she'd have been focused on her grades. He graduated and she didn't.

An idea slides between the two halves of his brain. "How about I ask Randall to get me in where he's working?"

She reminds him, "We still need rent money by tomorrow, or we're out of here."

A hundred dollars a week—that's the going rate at the Westfield Motel.

Tommy made three times that each week at the stamping plant. But his foreman, Gill Sullivan, is such an asshole—nobody in that place can stand to work for the guy. Tommy's the only one with balls big enough to just walk.

Melissa gives her shoulders a shrug, sending her pink bathrobe to the floor—the bathrobe Tommy bought her just last Christmas—exposing her bare body. It belongs to him, that milk-white skin, those small breasts shaped like two overturned teacups, that sparse tangle of hair where her legs meet—brunette, same as on her head.

Jealousy and anger compete with an emotion he'll never confess aloud.

"Why would he ask you to do this?" Tommy wonders aloud, watching his girl dress for her father's best friend.

"Fantasy," she says, "—how should I know what's inside his head?"

Tommy tries another angle. "Bet he won't be your dad's pal if word of this ever gets out."

Melissa dismisses his veiled threat without retort.

Black lace panties and matching bra hide her goodies. Blue jeans and a Rolling Stones concert t-shirt finish out her ensemble.

"I'll be home by nine," she promises, leaving him little more than a peck on the lips.

* * *

Tommy paces over the filthy mustard-yellow carpet, every so often tossing his gaze between musty-smelling pea-green curtains that keep the outside world from creeping inside the room.

Midnight.

Midnight, and no sign of Melissa.

Midnight, and that old pervert has probably been inside her all night.

"Gotta go get her," he tells himself, grabbing his car keys from the nightstand.

* * *

His Toyota finds refuge near the corner at the top of Canyon Drive. Well-to-do, the residents of this neighborhood. The sort of place Tommy's own parents live—though they'd not lift a finger to help him out. His fault, though. He's the one who chose Melissa over college.

He slips between two houses, stumbles onto the cement patio behind the home in question—the one where the dirty deed might still be in progress.

Does he really want to see such a thing?

Movement captures Tommy's attention; shadows dance against sheer drapes. Him—the one calling himself Melissa's godfather.

The scent of cinnamon incense passes through the open window. And music, too. Dave Brubeck's jazz.

And there he is, the man himself, strutting around in nothing but gray boxers. It's in that moment that his eyes fix on Tommy, the stupid boy standing on the patio peeking through an open window.

But the man doesn't call him on this intrusion; he offers his back, showing off the—

Tommy's own voice startles him. "What the hell…?"

Black—two of them!

And made of feathers!

"She's not here," the man says, extending those wings on his back. "And you shouldn't be here either."

Wings!

Real! Genuine! Wings!

Words and letters mingle on Tommy's tongue, tripping up the boy's intended line of questioning. "What are—?"

The man (Angel? Demon?) hollers, "Go!"

How Tommy got out of that backyard without breaking his own neck is one of those mysteries that shall forever remain.

* * *

"Where have you been?" Melissa asks, catching Tommy in the motel parking lot.

A single word slips past his lips. "Store."

She leans through the Toyota's window, presses a kiss to his lips. "I followed your suggestion and asked my parents for the money," she says, heading for their room. "I couldn't go through with that other thing; it'd feel like I was cheating on you."

"You would have been," Tommy proclaims, climbing from his car.

A job, she's saying, working in her father's office. "But that doesn't mean you're off the hook just because *I* have a job. I expect you to call Randall first thing in the morning."

"Wings," he announces. Says it aloud, searching her face for a clue.

Bewilderment, is what he finds.

She drops onto the bed. "Huh?"

"Never mind," he mumbles, falling into the familiar warmth of his girl. "Never mind."

Taking Lumps

Mrs. Lipke has only one breast. Cancer took the left one before they moved into our neighborhood a few years ago. She doesn't even try to hide it, either. There is no silicone, no falsie—not even a wad of toilet paper to add symmetry. She says it's a conversation starter, a means to get women to listen when she tells them the importance of searching for lumps.

I think it's just weird. I mean, who goes around with only one boob?

Anyway, I'm besties with her daughter, Toni—Antoinette. I'm at the Lipke house all the time, which means I have to be polite about the whole boob situation. Sometimes I stare at Mrs. Lipke's chest, imagining what it must look like where the left one used to be. Is there a big hole, like a crater mark on the moon, or is it all just a mess of scar tissue? She caught me eyeing her one time, and gave me the whole "check for lumps, young lady" spiel in front of Toni's brothers. I think she meant to embarrass me—which she did.

"She's gotta have *tits* before she can check for *lumps*, Ma!" Danny Lipke teased.

Mrs. Lipke corrected her oldest child. "*Breasts*, Daniel. We don't use filthy slang in this house. And stop picking on Carrie. It's not what a man does."

"I've *got* boobs," I said, thrusting my chest in Danny's direction.

"Barely a handful," Danny countered.

Danny's fifteen—a know-it-all. And he likes me, too. I can tell by the way he's always staring at me whenever I come over. And for saying I have no tits, he sure doesn't mind letting his eyes linger on my chest—sort of the way I do with his mother.

Toni and I bonded over a mutual hatred for One Direction. That's how we became besties almost two years ago. But even though we're united in our dislike for that stupid boy band, we don't really like the same kind of music—or much of anything else, for that matter. I listen to what my parents have always played: The Beatles, the Stones, Led Zeppelin. Toni prefers Taylor Swift and Katy Perry. She's starting sixth grade in the fall, I'll be in seventh. I'm blond, she's not.

Toni asks, "Are we sleeping in the tent tonight?"

I plop down beside her like a sack of potatoes dropped on the sofa in the Lipkes' family room. "How come we can't pitch the tent in *your* backyard?"

"Because I have brothers," she argues, issuing her stock excuse for why every time we camp out it's always going to be at my house.

My house is boring. I'm an only child—well, at least since my brother dropped out of school and moved in with his girlfriend last fall. The point is, there aren't any other kids at my house. The Lipke house is always full. It's where most of the neighborhood hangs out. They have a swimming pool and a basketball rim, ping pong and a pool table.

"You just want to hang out with Danny," Toni complains.

My denial rings flat, empty. "No I don't."

"Do so. He gets a boner every time you come over."

Danny hurtles the back of the sofa, snatches his sister in a chokehold, and works a serious nuggy into her head. "Erection, Toni. We don't use filthy slang in this house," he says.

Toni fights back—or at least tries to. "Let go, *spaz!*"

Like a boa constrictor, Danny's arm lays on the squeeze.

My brother, he's nothing at all like Danny. He never once gave me a nuggy, never caught me in a chokehold, either. One time, the first summer Toni's family moved into the neighborhood, Danny skipped a rock off the top of Toni's head, sending her to the hospital for stitches and a bald spot where the hair still doesn't look quite the same. Toni's younger brothers bide their time, just waiting for size to catch up with aspirations. She'll have her hands full then.

* * *

"I hate my stupid brother." She says it often enough to be believed.

But I don't believe her. "You'll laugh about it one day," I assure her.

"Nope. I won't."

"At least he knows you're alive. Paul never bothers to be a brother to *me*."

She unrolls her sleeping bag against the tent floor and sits pouting.

Toni's pretty when she pouts.

Then again, Toni's pretty *all* the time: long black hair, perfect white teeth, eyes like cool blue sky right after a good rain.

And a butt that has me convinced I could easily be into girls.

"Wanna make out?" I ask. It's ritual. Practice, we tell each other—for when we'll have boyfriends.

She's the only one who believes *that* story.

"Not tonight. Tonight, I just *wanna* be pissed off."

"Let it go," I say. "You're being a downer."

Wind gusts shake the tent, threatening to lift it—and us—into the night sky. A low rumble promises trouble before too long.

"I'm not sleeping out here if it's lightning." Toni lacks that sense of adventure found in most kids our age.

Dozens of Hello Kitty faces smile at us from my sleeping bag. Not a fan, mind you. It was a gift from a misinformed grandmother a few birthdays ago.

"Do you miss Paul?" Toni props her head against her pillow, eyes me with curiosity.

"Yes," I say. But then an image changes my mind for me. "No. He made my mom cry."

"Do you think he and Dori do it?"

"Duh! They live together. I bet they fuck every night."

Toni scrunches her nose at the notion. "Eew."

"Do you ever worry your mom will get cancer again?" I've asked her that question twice before. There's always the same answer.

"I won't worry about what I can't change." Thoughtful, that expression painting her face. "I just wish she'd get a boob implant. She's too lopsided."

I want to kiss her and feel the warmth of her soft lips, the moist darting of her tongue. But we won't be doing that. Not tonight. Toni's in one of her moods. It's like her head becomes filled with notions and ideas she's not willing to share with anybody.

Still, I share everything with her. I've never kept back a thought—no matter how stray it may be.

"Do you like Danny?" she asks.

It's a nervous thing, that shrug I offer. I say, "Maybe—a little."

But I don't—not really.

I like Toni.

"Boys are stupid," she announces, shedding her sleeping bag like a needless second skin. "—except for Andy Rakowski."

Andy is her dream boy, the one she imagines while kissing me.

Her hand finds mine, pulls me closer.

She dictates these moments.

Her kiss is always soft; her tongue tastes of mint toothpaste.

She's with Andy right now.

It comes in reverse, the rumble of thunder followed by a bright white flash.

"I'm going home," Toni says, shoving me away.

I won't try to stop her. It's no use when she has her mind made up.

She tosses words over her shoulder while departing. "We'll do it again tomorrow night."

I don't mind the lightning. Weather never bothers me. The way I see it, if lightning hit my tent, maybe I'd survive and be famous.

* * *

Alone, I lose myself in the wanderings of my thoughts. Maybe I won't be Toni's friend anymore. What if I start hanging out with girls in my own class, girls like Ashley Tobik or Shelly Cookman?

Girls of notable reputations.

Rumors of slumber party indiscretions made the rounds last New Year's Eve.

A double flash lights him up from behind, giving Danny that *Friday the 13th* menace.

"You alone?" he asks.

An abbreviated nod tips my head forward and back.

He wonders, "Where's Toni?"

"Home," I say.

"Lightning?"

Another nod, more vigorous this time.

Uninvited, Danny takes up residence on Toni's sleeping bag. He's wet from the rain but isn't bothered by it.

"Did she talk about me?"

"A little," I tell him. "Says you like me."

"You let her believe that?"

"Of course. I told you I'd never tell anybody."

Danny's gay, and I'm the only one he's ever told.

"She's never gonna give you what you want," he says, scooting closer to me.

"I know." It's all I can think of to say.

Dull yellow trickles into the tent from the back-porch light, illuminates Danny's dark gaze.

His tone comes low, a secret-filled hush. "You gonna let me see 'em?"

"See what?"

"Your tits."

"Why? You like boys."

"Curious, I suppose."

I don't even think about it; I just pull my nightshirt over my head and toss it behind me.

His touch is cold and wet, but comforting.

"Barely a handful," he teases. It's there in his eyes, that rare spark of seriousness. "If I ever decided to have a girlfriend, I'd want it to be you."

I believe him.

But all I can think to say is, "Same here."

We talk for an hour, maybe longer. Mostly about other kids in the neighborhood and what they'd think if they only knew Danny's secret. He wants to move to California after he graduates.

I want to go with him.

* * *

My mother is the one who wakes me at seven in the morning.

"Come inside, Carrie." She says it with a soothing tone—like the one she used when I was in bed with the flu last winter.

There's a police officer sitting at our kitchen table, a notepad in hand.

Have I seen Danny Lipke since yesterday afternoon?

An idea twirls through my head like a giddy ballerina drunk on the knowledge that she's the lead in *Swan Lake*. Did he decide California couldn't wait for graduation?

I can't bring myself to give him away, to rat him out.

"Last I saw him was yesterday at his house—before me and Toni came back here."

But joyful notions of Danny living in San Francisco or Los Angeles fade with news of the boy's body being found in Kinder Park, struck down by a random bolt of lightning sometime in the night.

* * *

Toni will never stay the night again. She'll forever fear the vulnerability required to take rest beneath an open sky. We'll forge our own paths in life, separated from a friendship that can't withstand such loss. I've become a sore memory to her, to the entire Lipke family. Our very neighborhood is now an open wound.

They'll move away before the school year begins. The loss of her firstborn will be too much for Mrs. Lipke, and cancer will return, defeating her this time, removing her from the world before the end of winter.

"Check for lumps," she'll say, right up to the end.

But it won't matter.

Life is full of lumps.

Came the Flood

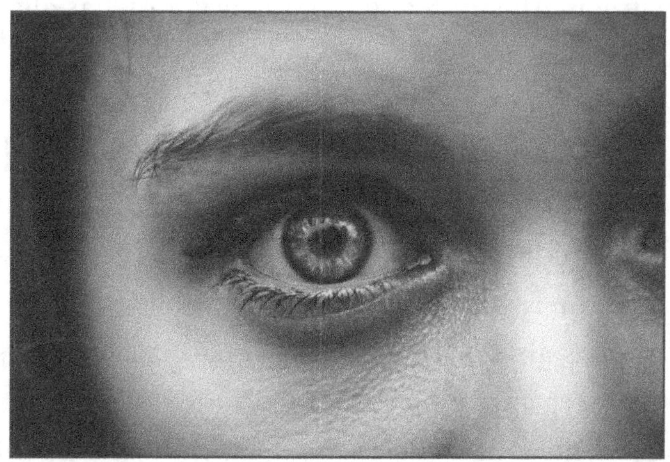

Imagine puffy white clouds the size of a grown man's fist, taking shape right in front of your face. Now imagine those same clouds forming shapes of numbers and letters—letters that never ever spell *any*thing. That's what *I* deal with every day. The numbers are the worst. Numbers are just naturally angry—the way they look, I mean. Numbers are all angles and sharp edges—except for 8. *Eight* is nice and rounded, unable to poke out an eye or stab a person in the back when she's not looking. And when numbers speak, they never have anything nice to say to me. They prefer subtlety, the way they whisper in my ear, where nobody but I can hear.

I know. This doesn't make sense to me, either.

I'd just turned ten when they first uttered that ugly word.

Schizophrenia.

Just saying it aloud leaves a copper-penny taste in my mouth. But that could just be the meds I'm supposed to take.

My name is Allison Kanga, but everybody has always just called me Roo.

Kanga-*roo*. Get it?

Schizophrenia is the diagnosis they laid against all those quirks and bad manners I'd gathered like some sort of crazy baseball card collection. Lots of colorful pictures—minus the stats on the reverse, of course.

And there's always a buzz in my head, an off-key sort of hum, usually teasing me with some vague melody that I can't quite ever make out—the meds again, or so I'm told. But how could anybody but me know for sure? See, I've always heard those songs—even before the rounds of Stelazine or Haldol or Trilafon.

I'm on Prolixin these days.

Dr. Severnsky, she's all right; she just digs too deep sometimes, always wanting to know what's going on inside my head.

I honestly didn't mean to bite her in our session last week. Besides, *six* told me to do it, so technically it's not even my fault.

The talk this week is about group homes and how would I feel about living in one. Pretty lousy, if you want to know the truth. Who wants to live with a bunch of schizophrenic assholes who talk to the air—the same way *I* do.

But I'm getting better. I swear I am.

Now, if only *six* would shut up and leave me alone, I just might learn to become normal and not stand out so much.

"I saw God once," I say. "He even talked to me."

Dr. Severnsky shifts in her chair. "You're avoiding the subject, Allison."

"He said, 'It's Friday. So why does your underwear say Tuesday?' Can you just imagine it? God even knows about our underwear."

Of course, Doc Severnsky couldn't possibly care any less about anything I have to say—unless I'm talking about those stupid group homes I'm supposed to be considering.

"You can't stay in the hospital forever, Allison."

"Why not?"

"We've been through this a dozen times already."

"And *you're* always the one talking. Just let me find an apartment of my own."

"Not a wise idea. You struggle under supervised situations. I can only imagine what would happen without assistance nearby."

I might succeed—that's what they're afraid will happen. See, I'll show them that I can do it on my own, and they'll all realize they aren't needed. I'm guessing it would be less than a year before all the other crazies catch on and opt out of this scam called psychiatry.

"I want a boyfriend," I announce.

"You aren't ready for a relationship."

"Am so. I get horny—same as every other girl."

"Sex isn't a relationship. You need to be stable for at least two years before you enter a relationship."

She sounds like my mother.

I hate my mother.

"What if I'm a lesbian?" I say it to get a response.

Dr. Severnsky isn't biting. "You're not a lesbian."

"Yeah. But what if I am?"

"The same rule applies. You need two years of stability before you date."

My mind wanders a lot. It's got to do with the chemicals in my brain. "God told me I'm not sick," I explain. "He said I'm just highly sensitive, astute."

"And the voices?"

"Just angels and demons, I suppose."

Dr. Severnsky's finger pushes her glasses up her nose before they end up in her lap. "You were an atheist just last year."

"People change. Lives gain meaning. God becomes real. Besides, He talked to me."

Then it appears yet again, that ugly discussion I cannot bear to engage.

"How do you feel about what your father did?" Dr. Severnsky asks, reading my face like an old issue of *The National Enquirer*. "What are your thoughts on him today?"

"Fuck him," I say—as I always do. "If he really loved me, he wouldn't have done it."

"It's a sickness, Allison."

"Bullshit. He knew what he was doing."

I hate it when she wags her stupid head back and forth, as if all I say or feel is wrong, wrong, wrong.

"Do you ever think about doing what he did?"

"Suicide?" I want a cigarette—even though I don't smoke. "Maybe I don't. Maybe I'm different from him."

"Do you still believe he passed it on to you?"

I'm certain of it. He gave me this disease then left me alone in the world.

"I hate him," I tell her.

"Hate is an awful strong word. Surely he left you with some fond memories."

Yes. That time we went to the ocean. Fort Lauderdale. We stayed in a hotel right on the beach. I don't think either of us heard any voices that were not our own during that week.

I ask the same question I've asked a million times since that long-ago trip. "What made you leave him?"

Dr. Severnsky shifts in her chair. "We're not here to talk about that."

"But you didn't just leave him, Mom. You left me as well. Left me to slide down the same hole as Dad."

"It's Doctor Severnsky in here, Allison."

"Yeah. Maybe that's why I struggle. Maybe you should have been my mother rather than being my shrink. Isn't there some sort of ethics issue with a situation like this one?"

There is, she reminds me. But she's the only one brave enough to sit alone in an office with me. Volatile behavior, they call it.

"I loved him," she says.

"That's why you left him and married this other dweeb."

"It's more complicated than that, Allison."

But I was there. We were a family and then we weren't. There's no getting around me on that one. I have memories. I know what transpired.

She says, "He became aggressive."

I say, "He was sick."

It always stops here, stuck at this point. She knows she failed him. I've heard it in her voice for years.

The star shrink that couldn't cure her one true love.

And I'm the one who found him at the end of that rope.

"I'm scared," I tell her. I've never uttered those words before.

"Of what?"

Letters and numbers shift and move through the shadows, finding cover in the darkened corners.

"I'll go." It's a statement of faith. I'll trust her on the group home.

Her hand finds my hand. Her body leans into me, offering comfort. It's a moment that we'll both forget once our session ends.

"I didn't mean to leave you behind." She says this every so often—more for herself than for me. It's a coping mechanism. I'd become just like him, and she could never have moved forward with that reminder hanging over her like a black dragon ready to spew its fire in those most inopportune moments.

The mom part of this relationship has passed. Dr. Severnsky pushes her glasses up her nose, and explains the procedure for getting me into a group home.

I don't really hate my mom.

I just say that sometimes.

It's a coping mechanism.

"Same time next week?" I say this after every session.

Dr. Severnsky's head tips a short nod. "Same time next week."

Dodging the Bullet

He'd gotten the drop on her and saw her first, those few critical seconds before she could discover him across the diner. It's those moments that allow for quick escape—should nerves begin to pull him apart at the seams. He wouldn't need that, though—not tonight, at least. She'd certainly changed. But twenty-odd years will do that to a person.

Jeremy Brickle is the one who told him she came here every Tuesday evening while her daughter took dance lessons two doors down.

Daughter!

How crazy is *that?*

Three children in all, Jeremy claimed. And it showed. She'd gone doughy around the middle. Streaks of gray mingled among the mostly brunette strands framing her round face. He could still see her, though, in her green-eyed gaze—that girl he'd once loved all those years ago.

"Wow," she said, picking him out from among the early dinner crowd. "Look at you."

Stiff hugs were exchanged, along with that awkwardly nervous handshake.

"How have you been?" he asked, dropping into the booth she'd saved for this very purpose.

A smile—or maybe a smirk—wrapped itself around the corners of her mouth. "Don't you ever age?" Her words fell heavily against the table lying between them.

Laugh lines, some women call them, those early wrinkles taking position at the edges of her eyes. Three kids and a nasty divorce, he figured the culprit to be. But the kids weren't his. Neither could the wreckage of the failed marriage be laid at his feet. No sir. He'd done just fine for himself: no kids, no ex-wife, nothing to hold him back from achieving what he set out to achieve.

"Still making music?" she asked, acting as if she didn't follow his career.

His fingers searched his breast pocket for the pack of cigarettes he knew would be there. "Producing other people, mostly," he explained, sucking smoke into his lungs.

"I don't listen much anymore—to music in general."

They'd been a couple for, what, five years? High school sweethearts with all sorts of big plans for the shared future they never found together. Suppose it had happened. Would they have toughed it out, remained intact as a couple? What would it have been like to wake up every morning, knowing there were children depending on him for their everything?

That was *her* dream, not his.

"We just lost interest in one another," she said of her failed marriage. "He went his way and I went mine. He's still a great father, though." Her green-eyed gaze fixed him tight. "What about you?"

"I'm doing all right for myself." It wasn't a lie, either. "I get steady work at the studio. I've built a good reputation as a producer."

"But you wanted to be the one writing the songs—and singing them," she reminded him. "I always expected to turn on the radio one day and there'd be your music coming through the speakers."

But that never happened.

Oh, he'd had his brush with celebrity. An album of his best work found release ten years earlier. But the label was regional, radio wouldn't touch it, and nobody bought the thing. Still, it's something he can point to with pride.

"I have it," she tells him—meaning his album. "I used to play it all the time."

Used to.

A list of excuses formed behind his eyes. She'd see through every one of them. She always had that knack. Reading him came easy to her.

"It's awful," he admitted. "—the album, I mean. That's why it failed. I'm not meant for that side of the business."

It's a subtle thing, her nod. She'd never actually agree with him on that point—but neither would she offer phony encouragement. She always allowed him to figure these things out for himself.

"Your voice is good. I always thought so." A sip from a glass of iced tea halted her review. She wouldn't offer too much more on the subject.

"I'm producing jingles," he blurted. "Commercial spots for radio. So, I guess I finally made the big time, eh?"

"And you drive a Lexus," she reminded him. "I got a seven-year-old Ford Taurus out of my marriage." Her smile, a thing most familiar, settled on her lips. "And I got three wonderful children as well. That was always my dream. Remember how I used to always say we'd have three kids—?"

"And we'd baby the middle child, since we were both neglected middle kids." He remembered those talks as if they'd never stopped having them. "Well, do you?—baby the middle one, I mean?"

"Spoiled rotten, that one."

Small talk ate into most of the remaining time. Much of their past remained buried, left alone, as if disturbing it might change lives—at least hers.

She didn't want change.

She didn't want the past.

Her dreams came true—even if the marriage part didn't work out.

"Lung cancer," he said. "Maybe a year left—though cancer doesn't exactly follow a doctor's prognosis."

No tears. Not even a look of shock.

"I always told you to quit smoking," she reminded him.

That had been one of the reasons they eventually split. He saw it as her wanting to change him. He rebelled and slept with her best friend.

He asked, "You happy?"

Her nod took the place of words.

"Well good. I'm glad to know that," he said.

"Why?"

A shrug lifted his shoulders. "Don't know. It just makes me feel better knowing—"

"Knowing you didn't ruin my life?"

His turn to nod.

Her words came with assurance. "Not a chance."

He'd envisioned this very moment a thousand times in the years since they found that place apart from one another. It always followed a pattern. She'd look at him with longing. Maybe a little envy tossed into the mix. He'd know—just know it in his heart—he could have her back with little more than a word or two. She'd practically beg him to save her from the miserable life she'd been forced into simply by losing him. *He* mattered most to her—at least in his daydreams.

But, she didn't need him. Hell, she didn't even want him. What use did she have for a man who would be dead inside of a year? In her world, she wouldn't change a thing.

Pity hijacked her countenance. *Pity*—minus the sadness of course. She didn't even know him anymore. She couldn't be moved by his plight. What they'd once had, that life they'd dreamed of creating together—those people no longer existed. They didn't die. They just ceased being.

She's the one who rose first. "Well, it's been nice seeing you again," she said, extending her hand, as if they'd only just met for the first time.

"Do you ever wonder—?"

"Never."

It hung there in the air between them, that finality. The starkness of the present erased most of the past—or at least scuffed it up pretty good.

The night air nipped at his hands as he slid the key into the door of his Lexus.

Maybe he'd gone there to silently gloat, to judge her on her fading looks and failing life. Dodging the bullet, he imagined.

Ah, but he wasn't the one who knew to duck.

When We Were Kids

I saw you again today. You were younger than the last time I set eyes on you. It happens that way sometimes. You were mowing the lawn in front of some house I didn't recognize. I doubt you did either.

It's the third time in a month that I've seen you cutting grass or jogging or playing in that park where we hung out when we were kids. You were always on the baseball diamond—even now. I suppose it has something to do with the uniforms. The colors are always different, but the style hasn't changed in thirty-odd years.

Dana Rickleman still talks about you whenever I run into her at the Winn-Dixie. Well, she's not Dana *Rickleman* these days. Neither is she hot anymore. She married Donnie Soba fifteen years or so ago, had a kid, put on more than a few pounds, and ended up deciding she's a lesbian. But maybe we already knew that way back when. Remember how she used to say Becky Fordham was enough to turn her?

Speaking of Becky, her younger brother Todd is gone. He went to Iraq during the Gulf War and never came back. He stepped on the wrong spot and left nothing behind but his dog tags. Becky turned into a boozehound after that one. Last I heard, she'd been in and out of Burnside Psychiatric Hospital.

The old neighborhood has completely changed. You wouldn't recognize it now. All those families we knew back then no longer live there. Kids grew up and went off to college, got married, chased careers out of state. Parents became grandparents, got old, retired, moved to Florida, and died. I drove through there a few months ago. Not a single familiar face among those I saw. Our old house is long gone. The family that bought it from Mom and Dad, after I moved out, lost it to fire. They rebuilt on the lot, but the house looks nothing like the original. And there are trees where there weren't any before. Crazy how that works, huh?

I'm sorry if it sounds like I'm rambling. I don't mean to. I've had a lot on my mind since, well, you know. I still struggle with things, Adam. It's always there in the front part of my mind, where it often blocks out my view of the world around me. I think that's why Mallory and I got a divorce. She saw those issues, tried to help me, but in the end, she just had to let it all go. It's not her fault. Even Mom says she's surprised Mallory didn't leave me a lot sooner—and you know how Mom was always my biggest cheerleader.

I won't lie to you. I've thought about it more times than I dare count. It's usually when I'm driving alone, just as the sun dips below the horizon, taking the sky from pink to orange to purple, and that day smacks me in the face all over again, the pain growing only stronger with the passing of time. The way I'd do it, I'd aim my car at some far away tree, mash the gas pedal to the floor, race toward it, and be done. But then I'd hear your annoying voice calling me a selfish little prick—the way you always did when we were kids.

When we were kids . . .

There's so much hurt wrapped around those four simple words.

When we were kids, we dreamed of playing Major League Baseball for the Atlanta Braves.

When we were kids, the only thing important to us was being able to stay outside for an hour or two after the streetlights came on.

When we were kids, we went everywhere on our bikes—and we never got tired of it.

Speaking of bikes, do you remember that time we decided we were going to train for the Tour de France? We spent that entire summer riding all over hell's half acre, thinking that's all it took to win that stupid race. In your version, you and I would finish in first and second place. Of course, our versions differed as to which finished where. In my head, I was always the victor. And the prize money, well, that was spent a thousand different ways. Always on something foolish or needless—it would mostly be squandered on selfish desires. Mom would rein us in by taking charge of our fabled earnings. Into the bank, it would have to go. After all, we had college to think about.

I worry about Mom since Dad died. It's not that I doubt her ability to carry on and live a productive life; she's done that well enough in the three years since. It's that profound sadness that envelops her when a birthday or anniversary or an old TV show worm their way into her cocoon, threatening to pull her out before she's good and ready to deal with life as a changed species. She went out to dinner with Mr. Griffith from the church once—but that felt too much like adultery, essentially killing any notion of date number two. I just don't want her to be miserable. It's just her and me now, from our nuclear family. You always hated that term. You used to say it made you think that families could explode, taking entire cities with them. There'd be a mushroom cloud over our town—and it would mostly be Dad.

I miss his yelling about this and that.

Okay. So, here's the thing: I've never told anybody about that day. I never even told Mallory—and I told her a ton of major important things. I just can't seem to make myself speak those words out loud. But I have to. It's wrecking me, brother.

It was an accident. I swear on it.

I'm the one who locked you in the shed that day.

The day you died.

I did it. It was supposed to be a joke—a prank. I padlocked the door, expecting you to pitch a fit at being locked in. I'd leave you in there for a few minutes before letting you out. Then you'd sock me in the shoulder, and we'd have a laugh about it. But Donnie Soba showed up with a pocketful of fire crackers. I didn't mean to leave you in the shed. I meant to unlock the door. I got sidetracked.

I didn't know it could get so hot inside there.

I swear on it, Adam.

It was Dad who found you. He'd called the police after you failed to come inside once the street lights came on. He stomped around the living room, threatening to ground you for a hundred years, every so often yelling your name out into the night. Once Carson came on, the police were called. They drove the neighborhood, spotlights trained in the dark corners, searching for a wayward boy. I don't know what it was that made Dad go out to the shed. It didn't occur to me until he grabbed the key for the lock.

"I killed you, Adam." There. I said it out loud.

It doesn't make it easier.

I'm not just a killer. I'm the guy who killed his own brother.

I need to hear your voice, Adam. I need to know your thoughts on my transgression. Where are you? What do you see? What do you know? Have you been watching these thirty-odd years? Is everything I tell you already known?

Have you seen God?

Does He hate me?

Sometimes it's like coming down with a cold. My body aches, my head throbs, and I can't bring myself to get out of bed. It's as if joy ceased to exist when you left. But I know that's not true. Other people still experience joy and happiness and laughter. I've heard it. I've seen it with my own two eyes. I've just never grabbed hold of it for myself—no matter how hard I try.

There really is no need for you to worry. Notions of wrapping my car around a tree are greatly exaggerated. I can't do that to Mom. Neither can I put myself in front of God before my proper ending. For all I know, I'll have to continue on well past the century mark, carrying the years as a burden.

Can you put in a word for me—the way you did when we were kids?

But would a simple word really count for anything?

I'm the reason you died, Adam.

Please forgive me.

Please.

Maybe it's desperation that has me hearing your voice.

"Let it go, twerp."

It comes audibly to me, as if you're standing right beside me, speaking it directly into my ear.

My left ear.

"Is that you, Adam?" I ask it aloud, hoping for more.

But there's nothing else.

"Tell me again—just once more."

I think of Mom. Of telling her. Of unburdening my soul.

I won't, though. I cannot.

It's you I needed to tell.

It was always you.

And tonight, you heard me.

Of that, I am certain.

My burden isn't gone just yet, but it sure feels lighter.

"Thank you, Adam."

Songs of the Lost

Curtis Dinwitty found himself a few days shy of his tenth birthday in the summer of 1965. Still, he lacked that hum of expectation, which had occurred with each of the previous eight markings of his years on planet Earth. This one would be different. This one would be the very first such marking since the loss of his mother.

Curtis allowed himself tears early in the morning, while still in bed, just before the sun breached the horizon at the far edges of the cotton field across the road from the Dinwitty house. He couldn't chance his father seeing tears on a boy. No sir. That'd mean the strap. He'd had enough of that heavy leather thing to last him well into his adult years—especially since his mama passed. "Men don't cry," his daddy was fond of saying. Even his baby sister Olive didn't cry around their father. Olive Dinwitty wore a peculiar look in her eyes that hinted at an old soul dwelling inside her six-year-old body. When she spoke, even grown-ups sometimes marveled at the wise sayings she might insert into a moment. Their mama always claimed the girl would be the first woman on the Supreme Court of the United States. Olive just knew how to keep the world around them from spinning out of control.

Curtis had things needing done. Namely, there were those walnuts that had fallen from the trees out back after all that recent wind. Mister Logan down at the market paid a quarter a pound. Curtis reckoned at least two pounds lay beneath those ancient trees. He had to get them up and into town before his father got to them first. He slipped into his denim overalls and crept from his bedroom, hoping to avoid all those creaky floorboards that might tell on him. And he hoped to be out the door before Olive knew what he was up to. She'd just beg and plead for a chance to tag along.

* * *

"Three pounds' worth, Curtis," said Mister Logan. "That's a pretty good haul today." Mister Logan was a tall, thin man with a bald spot on the top of his head. Rumor had it he'd been grazed by a bullet during the war in Korea, and that's what kept the hair from returning. "You want credit or just the money?"

"Just the money, please," Curtis informed him. The boy had things to do, and a little loose change in his pocket just made it easier to get what he wanted most.

The grocer handed over three shiny quarters, offered him his choice from a variety of candy in the glass case. He chose a peppermint stick—for Olive, not himself. A bribe went a long way in keeping his baby sister from yapping on about how Curtis had snuck off first thing in the morning—without so much as inviting her along.

* * *

One block down and two streets over from the market lived an old black man named William Calhoun Jenkins Jr. Most folks just called him lazy. Curtis called him Sir. Jenks—as the man himself preferred—had been around for many years. He'd seen the best and the worst in mankind. Still, he never let anger or hatred poison his soul.

Curtis approached the house from the backyard, squeezing through an opening in the old wooden fence. If seen, there'd be questions as to what business he might have with Jenks. Some folks would feel it their place to tell his father. That would only lead to the strap and lots of yelling. They didn't know Jenks the way Curtis knew the man.

The boy gained footing on that rickety porch and laid a knock against the door. Jenks had no family in the area. His only son moved off to Chicago back before the Second World War and never again set foot in Georgia. Old Jenks had never even set eyes on his own grandchildren.

Jenks peered through the window. His eyes lit up like they were taking in family—or an least an old dear friend. "Hello there, Mister Curtis," he said, stepping out on that porch. "What can I do for you this fine morning?"

Curtis thrust his arm out, three shiny quarters in hand. "I got this for you, Sir."

A knowing smile lifted the sagging corners of the man's mouth. "Seems to me like it might just shape up to be a fetching day." Jenks took the money in hand and nodded for the boy to have a seat on the steps. It wouldn't take long for things to transpire. Curtis would wait there while Jenks walked the block to the market. He'd reappear ten minutes later with a bottle of strawberry wine in a brown paper sack. Two or three quick pulls from the bottle, is all the priming it took for Jenks to retrieve his old Martin guitar.

That's why Curtis came to see the man.

Jenks slid an empty glass pill bottle onto his left ring finger and set about playing the finest slide guitar Curtis ever heard. He'd sing songs that told tales of long days and short nights working in the fields. Then he'd segue into a lament concerning some woman who broke his heart long ago. The beauty of the playing, that aged voice, and those words—that's what kept Curtis coming back. That's what made risking the strap worth it.

It had been their routine going back to before the boy's mama had died. Back when his father still worked at the textile plant. Curtis would gather up the walnuts, turn them into money, and give it to Jenks—just to hear that amazing music. His mother understood. She enjoyed music just as much as Curtis did. His father was another story altogether.

The man didn't care much for music—especially blues music as sung by an old black man.

Songs poured from the elderly gentleman as if his very soul opened up and had its say on the affairs of a lengthy life. Between the songs—and the sips from his bottle—Jenks offered stories from early in his life. He regaled the boy with tales of playing blues in clubs and saloons from here to Chicago. Told how he'd always kept a single-shot Derringer in his boot—just in case. He'd crossed paths with Robert Johnson himself once, in a club in St. Louis. He claimed they'd played a couple of songs together.

"But that man could not play worth a lick, this being a time before he met the Devil at the crossroads," Jenks explained.

Jenks had to be nearing eighty years in this world. Still sharp for such an age. But this particular morning saw him haggard and moving at a pace slower than usual. Curtis chalked it up to too much wine too early in the day.

"How's your daddy?" the old man asked.

Curtis shoved his shoulders into a shrug, said, "Mean and drunk, mostly."

"It's just the way of some men, Son. When a married fella loses his wife, a piece of himself goes into the grave with her."

"But he's been this way since I can recall. My mama's the one kept him in line all those years."

Jenks took another pull from his bottle, asked after Olive.

"She's the one doing best of us all, I think," Curtis told him. "She's tough—for being just six."

Jenks offered a knowing nod. He'd lost his own wife when his son was just four. The boy adapted in ways even a grown man could not.

"I reckon it changed my son from who he was meant to be," he explained, "though that's something we can't really know for sure."

Jenks proceeded with a couple more songs before ending his back-porch show. He put away his old guitar until the boy returned in another week's time with a few more quarters as enticement. He pulled himself up from those steps and grimaced in pain the way he had not done before.

"You okay, Sir?" Curtis asked.

"Be just fine, Son. Be just fine."

* * *

"Where you been all morning, Curty?" Olive asked from her perch atop a low-hanging limb of the tree smack in the middle of their front yard. She already knew the answer without him telling her so. She also knew to expect that peppermint stick he slipped into her small hand.

"Where's Daddy?" he asked, gauging the situation.

"In the kitchen, making lunch."

"Does he know I've been gone?"

"Nope. I told him you been doing chores. And since I did them for you, you owe me, Curty."

He tipped his head in agreement. He'd wash the dishes after lunch, he told her.

"And take the wash off the line when it's dry," she added, making no pretense at negotiation.

Olive jumped off the limb and landed at the boy's feet. She wore a pair of his overalls he'd outgrown some years ago. Their mother held onto all his old clothes in hope of having another boy someday. A brother would have been preferred over a sister. Not that he minded having a sister. Olive lent a softness to his life since their mother had passed. She acted tough, sure, but he knew the real person inside. When late-night thunderstorms chased the girl from her room, she'd always end up in *his* bed—even when their mother was still alive. She found comfort in her big brother; and Curtis, well, he took comfort in knowing that.

"Why are you wearing my old clothes?" he asked her, heading for the small barn out back. "You want folks thinking you're a tomboy?"

"Maybe I am," she retorted. "Besides, Daddy won't let me climb trees in a dress. He says it's not proper."

"What's *he* know about proper?"

"Probably nothing, I suppose."

Bessie the cow stood sentry in her stall inside the barn, eyeing the two kids with indifference.

Curtis asked, "Did you milk her already?"

"Told you I did all your chores." Olive slipped her hand into her brother's. "She didn't even fuss with me." She favored their mother, with her brunette hair and blue eyes. She even had the same small nose and delicate chin.

His arm went around her. He kissed the top of her head—just the way their mother used to do. "Don't suppose he's going to bake a cake this year, do you?"

"Daddy?" Olive's laughter came almost cruel in its delivery. "You don't want to eat a cake *he* baked. He can hardly fry an egg. I'm surprised we ain't starved just yet."

Curtis corrected her. "Haven't starved."

"Mama's not here no more. It doesn't matter how I talk."

She'd do that from time to time, just slip into poor speaking habits. Curtis took it as Olive's way of rebelling against their loss—at least that's how Miss Frish, his teacher, explained it to him. People grieve in different ways.

"Why can't we ride Bessie around the yard?"

"Because she's not a horse."

Olive dropped onto a hay bale and found her brother's gaze. "You still going to hear Jenks play his guitar?"

"You can't tell Daddy," Curtis told her. "I don't feel like getting the strap again."

"I wanna go next time," she demanded.

"Can't."

"Why?"

"It's only for men."

"Then why do *you* get to go?"

* * *

"You get that cow milked?" Arthur Dinwitty asked his son.

Curtis took the plate of fried potatoes from him. "Yes, sir," he said. "Milk's in the icebox."

"Didn't ask where it was." Arthur was in a mood. He'd had a few nips from that bottle he kept stashed beneath the kitchen sink—the bottle he was certain neither of his kids knew about. "Gotta keep her milked, so she don't burst."

"Would she really burst, Daddy?" Olive asked, chewing a mouthful of potatoes.

"Course she would, puddin' pie. We can't afford to let that happen."

They couldn't afford to keep the cow, neither. She ate up more in hay than she gave in milk.

"I think she's drying up," Curtis said.

"What, you a farmer now? You know these things how?"

Curtis hated these moments. They never had these conversations when his mother sat at that very dinner table.

His father fixed him in that off-kilter sort of way he'd developed over the previous year. It's a look that says he's not sure about this boy claiming to be his son. "You leave the knowing stuff to me. I been tending cows for longer than you been alive."

But it wasn't *cows* any longer. It was just old Bessie.

Curtis worked up his courage, said, "My birthday's coming soon."

Nothing. Not even a look from his father.

"Aunt Lottie will bake you a cake, Curty," Olive promised. "She'll have us over after church this Sunday."

Arthur slid his glance toward his daughter. "That's right, puddin' pie. Aunt Lottie will fix it up right."

And she would, too. Lottie was his mother's younger sister. She's been there from the first days of Curtis's life. She even offered to take in both children after their mother's untimely end. Of course, Arthur had other ideas that didn't include anybody but him raising his own kids.

The man found Curtis with a hard look. "Why don't you shovel up after Bessie when you're done with lunch. Got shit two feet deep in her stall."

Olive spoke up. "I'll help you, Curty. That way it won't take long."

Arthur shook his head, stuffed the last bite of his hamburger into his mouth. "You're going to stay inside with me, puddin' pie."

Curtis saw it, that glance of understanding that passed between daughter and father. He grabbed his empty plate and took it to the kitchen.

Their muffled conversation trickled into earshot.

Arthur's voice came hushed, low. "Did you take a bath this morning like I told you?"

Olive's voice sounded smaller than usual. "Yes, sir."

"Go on, then. Go to my room. I'll be right in."

It's one of those things without reference points. Thoughts walked through Curtis's mind, offering notions over what it might be that those two shared. He imagined spirited games of Candyland or Old Maid taking place behind his father's closed bedroom door. Or maybe they just talked. Olive could easily carry a solid conversation with grown-ups, like she'd been here for forty years.

Arthur brought his and Olive's plates into the kitchen, set them in the sink. "Go on now," he ordered his son. "Go do as I told you."

Burning with a curiosity he'd never known, Curtis slipped out the back door. Instead of heading for the barn and Bessie's stall, he hooked a right and skirted the side of the house where a window looked in on his father's room. Shrubs his mother planted several summers ago concealed his mission.

He raised up on the tip of his toes and tossed his gaze inside. It took a moment for his sight to adjust against the shadows. The pale white of Olive's bare bottom is the first thing his eyes and mind agreed upon. The girl herself stood at their mother's vanity, eyeing her nakedness in the round mirror. She climbed on the bed and crawled to its center, where she lay down, waiting.

Waiting for what?

Arthur crept inside and shut the door behind him. He spoke words to Olive, his tone kind and playful and gentle. Their meaning wasn't so clear, those words—at least not to a boy standing beneath the window—but Olive, she let go a giggle, as if some funny man on Ed Sullivan just told a joke.

It's his legs that moved Curtis from that window to the barn, though his mind had a thing or two to do with his retreat. Suppose he witnessed a sight that stayed stuck inside his head? And suppose it was a thing that would always be replayed every time he looked at his sister? No, sir. A boy doesn't need recollections like *that.*

He guessed it an hour by the time Olive bounded into the barn, those overalls covering her body again, acting like nothing odd had transpired.

"I can help now," she offered.

Curtis dropped onto a hay bale. "It's done already."

Olive approached him. There wasn't a thing out of the ordinary with this girl. It's like she'd only been inside watching TV. "Well, I say we ride Bessie."

The smell of his mother's perfume filled his head. "Why are you wearing it?" he asked, trying hard not to sound demanding.

"Daddy says I could."

"What did he do to you in there?"

Her blue-eyed gaze narrowed down hard on him. "He didn't do *nothing!* And you ain't part of it, so you don't get to know."

He'd trapped the girl in her own words. "If he didn't do anything, then why can't I know?"

Olive was small but strong. Her tiny hand clamped down over his mouth. "Don't you talk about it," she demanded. "Don't you say anything more about nothing. I just look like Mama, is all. Daddy misses her."

The happening lay unspoken for the remainder of the evening. They watched their regular shows for a Thursday night: *Lassie*, *My Favorite Martian*, *Ed Sullivan*, and *Bonanza*. Curtis sat in his usual place on the sofa; Olive lay on the floor in front of the Philco television in her nightgown. Their father, he had fallen asleep in the recliner. To those two, nothing was different, off kilter, or removed from what had been there before. Curtis, he just couldn't let it alone. He may not have known what happened in his father's bedroom, but he sure knew it wasn't a good thing.

* * *

"Is she hurt?" Jenks asked.

Curtis sat on the old man's back porch and shared with him all he'd seen. "She acts like nothing happened, like I only imagined what I saw."

"Well," he said, scratching at the white whiskers on his chin, pondering some wise saying he might drop into the conversation. "Olive is a tough girl. I reckon whatever happened, she aims to keep it from burdening *you*."

"But *I'm* the big brother! *I'm* supposed to look after *her*."

Jenks understood. His dark eyes went clear—clearer than they'd been in years. "You still got that auntie lives in the area?"

He did. She lived just twenty minutes away by car.

"Then tomorrow, you gonna bring Olive over here, like as if you just stopping by for some blues."

Curtis's head tipped a subtle nod. "Then what?"

"That ain't for you to know."

* * *

The sheriff's the one found Curtis there at the old black man's back porch, Olive seated beside him. They'd taken

Jenks into custody, the man said—though he didn't say why. The law man left that to their Aunt Lottie.

"Just knocked on the door and shot your daddy in the head," Lottie explained once she put Olive to bed. "You two will be staying here with me."

Curtis sat on the sofa, his eyes fixed on the television, though he couldn't name the program playing out in living color. "What about Daddy?"

"He'll live," she said. "But he won't ever be the man he was. He's going to be staying at the county home for some time. He can't even speak his own name anymore." Lottie switched off the television and cornered the boy's gaze. "Why do you suppose that old black man shot your daddy, Curtis?"

A shrug fell empty and unconvincing. He told his aunt what he'd seen through the window. "I told it to Jenks—but I didn't expect him to go and try to kill Daddy."

"He's dying, Curtis. Mister Jenkins has cancer. They don't reckon he'll be around long enough for a trial."

The boy felt worse for the old colored man than he did for his own father. And he figured there must be something wrong in his way of feeling—just one of those gut notions. But maybe God would understand his reasoning. Had he not told what he saw, his father might be asleep in the recliner at that very moment.

"Jenks did it to help," he told his aunt. "Bet he used his old Derringer, too."

"Well, then," she said, tousling his hair, "that makes the old man a hero." She tossed a nod toward the kitchen. "How about we get started on baking somebody a birthday cake?"

Gifted

Griffin Loomis climbed from his car beneath a high Iowa sun, and leaned with pride against the left front fender. Everybody had seen it by now, that beautiful '57 Bel Air, brand spanking new, fresh off the dealer's lot. Red on white. Red leather interior. Chrome hubcaps.

Nothing can top a Chevy for graduation.

Nothing at all.

The Kodak dangled from its cord around his neck, lens cap off, camera at the ready for yet another ending—or beginning, depending on how one chose to view the moment.

The boys gathered first, the way they always did, eight or nine of the little bastards, all lined up along the sidewalk in front of Roosevelt Elementary, each hoping to get noticed, each praying to be the chosen. Sixth graders, mostly—though

Timmy Maxwell, he had to be a grade or two short on that end of the stick.

But give the kid credit for aiming so high.

The girls, they followed behind her, mostly tagging along for sake of appearance: *Look at me! I'm walking with her!* Others, those obsequious few, might spend summer break as her inner circle.

Griffin raised the Kodak, pressed his eye against its viewfinder, and aimed for the boys.

"She's not perfect," he told them, hoping to capture their stunned disbelief.

Mikey Nixon's the one who spoke up. "Close enough to perfection as *we're* gonna see."

Griffin lowered the camera and shoved away from his car. "See," he began, moving closer to his kid sister's admirers, "it's horny little monkeys like you that give her an inflated sense of herself. You're always putting her on a pedestal."

Defiance grabbed at Jeff Knapp, jerked his spine straight as a fence post. "She's the prettiest girl in Iowa," he pronounced.

Griffin counted all those glaring holes in the boy's proclamation and reached for the biggest one. "There's probably a million people in the state," he explained, building his case. "You haven't *seen* enough to make that sort of claim. Besides, true beauty lies in the flawed, not the flawless."

But attentions shifted, and gears changed, eyes refocused on the girl herself. She cut a swath through a crowd near the school's main entrance. She'd stop here and there, either speaking or listening—depending on the prevailing wind.

Mikey Nixon, jockeying for first dibs, said, "Here she comes!"

Griffin raised the Kodak again, found her in its view. "Penelope farts," he announced to the throng of boys. "A lot." His fingers twisted at the lens, laid clear the unfolding scene. "Never says excuse me, either."

Penelope split from the crowd, sloughed off the tag-alongs, dispensed with her closest friends, and touched down alone on the sidewalk.

A corn-silk blond ponytail, poodle skirt, white blouse, and saddle shoes—that's all those boys cared about. They knew nothing of the angry pink gash along her right side where she'd lost a kidney at age five. Or the fact that the one remaining kidney began to fail just four years later. This, the result of bad genes passed from mother to daughter.

Griffin opened the shutter, captured the image of his baby sister. "Lots of flaws, boys," he said, making reiteration on the subject.

Penelope slowed her pace, inspected the boys the way President Eisenhower would his troops when he'd been a general. Her jaw worked at a wad of bubble gum with singular determination.

"Mikey Nixon," she pronounced, sizing up her eager suitor.

The boy's smirk suggested *he'd* be the lucky one, the chosen to walk her home.

Penelope's fist doubled down like a small stone in David's sling—a true southpaw, this girl.

Griffin aimed the Kodak; its aperture winked, immortalizing the punch that dropped Mikey like a sack of unwanted puppies destined for the river.

The boy sat up; a crimson flow gushed from his nose.

Penelope stood over him the same way Marciano would a fallen foe. "*That's* for calling me *Penny* after I warned you not to," she informed him.

Mikey tried for an apology, but failed to find his voice.

Penelope dismissed her wounded Romeo and sidled up to Timmy Maxwell.

"My brother's here," she told her would-be chosen, "so you can't walk me home." She plucked the well-worked hunk of gum from her mouth. "But you can have this."

Young Timmy eyed the pink wad glistening with her saliva.

And like one of the faithful on a pilgrimage, the boy opened his mouth and received communion at the hand of Roosevelt's most coveted.

Penelope peeled off toward the waiting car, left her gathering behind.

"Same as a kiss," said Timmy, chomping that spent treat.

The others disagreed. "Is not."

* * *

"How are you feeling?" Griffin asked, pulling away from the curb. She didn't need to answer. He could read her like last Sunday's paper.

Penelope slid across the seat, tucked up tight to her big brother, and rested her head against his shoulder. "Do you think it will work?"

"I do—but like Doctor Fetzer says, it's still a new idea," he reminded her.

"I'm scared. Scared for the both of us."

Griffin downshifted and angled the Chevy into the driveway. He was scared, too—but not for himself.

* * *

"You'll have the entire summer to lie around and recover," Agnes Loomis told her daughter over dinner.

Penelope picked at the heap of mashed potatoes in the center of her plate. "Suppose I die during the thing?"

"Don't be morbid, Kitten." Harold Loomis didn't like such talk from his youngest child. But he'd grown accustomed to the reality of the situation. She really could die—whether she goes through with it or not. And she'd go through with it. That had already been decided—by Penelope herself.

Griffin offered his own comfort. "At least this time you won't have to go through it alone. I'll be lying right beside you."

"Doctor Fetzer says it hurts worse for the one giving than the one getting," Agnes reminded her only son.

Didn't matter to him. He'd gladly give her both kidneys—if that's what it took.

* * *

June 10th was the chosen date. Then it became June 20th after Penelope developed a fever. Too risky, Doctor Fetzer determined. June melted into July, and on the night every kid in the United States waved sparklers like pom-poms in celebration of another American birthday, Penelope and Griffin Loomis entered Baptist Memorial Hospital with the intention of giving the girl her life back.

There were always setbacks where surgeries like this were concerned. The night of July 4th proved to be no exception. Harold Loomis sat in the hospital room with his children, assuring them of those things on which he had no business speaking. He held no real understanding of the future and what it might hold. But it's the thing a father does—even a fib can do good, if well placed.

Agnes Loomis hadn't been able to make this trip. The remaining kidney in her own body threatened mutiny, as it had so many times throughout her life. Her own mother had lost the great kidney battle when Agnes was only twelve years old. She married straight out of high school, got pregnant within a month of their nuptials. That child, a girl, didn't live to see five years. Griffin arrived two years later, healthy and without the bad genes. Penelope made her appearance seven years after, bringing with her that horrible curse.

But times had changed. Transplants became possible for those with the means—and Harold Loomis had those means.

Both children were prepped for the surgery. Together in the same theater they spoke of remembrances. Family stories were brought up, like favorite episodes from much-loved

TV programs, reminders of who they are—lest either should forget.

The anesthesiologist completed his part of this new ritual. Penelope nodded off first—but only by a few seconds.

* * *

It would take some time before they'd know anything for certain, the doctors explained to Harold Loomis.

"These are exciting times," Doctor Fetzer said.

Agnes Loomis held her daughter's hand, assuring the girl that all would be just fine.

Parents will do that. It's just what they do—even when they're uncertain.

"You're going to grow up and meet a boy someday," Agnes told Penelope, as if reading tea leaves over a table in a dark back room on the wrong side of town. "And you'll have children of your own."

"What if they get sick?" Penelope asked.

"These are exciting times." Those were the words Agnes grabbed hold of—even as the blipping machine in her son's room fell into an urgent beep.

Words like "cardiac arrest" fluttered through the air like moths in search of light.

* * *

"Almost died, son," Harold Loomis told the boy. "They had to shock your heart to restart the thing."

Agnes wept at the idea of losing another child—especially the healthy one.

But there'd be no such loss on that day. God and science saw fit to keep the Loomis family intact—at least for the time being.

"Exciting times," Doctor Fetzer repeated. "Exciting times indeed."

Looking for Lucy

They'd once been in love. Even they themselves admitted that much. That's how Vrable came to be. But things change, feelings fade, and eyes begin to wander. So, Vrable remained an only child to the soon-to-be-former Mr. and Mrs. Tambor.

Moving to the city was his mother's idea. His father, well, he'd keep the house. After all, it had been in his family for generations—going all the way back to the turn of the last century. It just wouldn't seem right kicking him out of what rightfully belongs to *him*. Still, the idea of leaving country living for New York City gave the boy anxiety.

"Nothing to be afraid of," his mother assured him.

"Not afraid," he promised—though that was a lie.

Vrable's mother lived in the city while in college. She never graduated, though. She met Mr. Tambor, and after a night of too much wine and equal measures of passion, the former Betty Stanton found herself pregnant and in love—though now she refers to it as poor judgment brought on by infatuation. Nevertheless, the two young steadies married and settled down on the Tambor family farm. Vrable arrived some months later.

But after ten years of marriage, one of them strayed. Vrable hadn't been able to decipher which parent transgressed, but almost certainly it was his mother. It's that guilty nature she'd nurtured the entire time he'd known her.

They downsized into a small two-bedroom apartment in Brooklyn, nothing at all like the stately four-bedroom farmhouse in which he'd spent his nearly ten years of life. Wide open spaces and giant barns had been his daily living. And his pony called Ghost. He'll miss Ghost more than he'll miss his father. He loves his dad, to be sure. But, well, being caught in the middle of both parents left Vrable wanting—needing—time apart from one or the other.

He'd seen her sitting on the front stoop that first day they arrived, a small girl, most likely the same age as Vrable—nine or ten, give or take a few months. Dark hair framed a cute face. A trail of freckles lay across her tiny nose, as if God Himself sprinkled them there—just as an afterthought. She sported a pair of yellow shorts and a white t-shirt that read *Give a Hoot, Don't Pollute.*

"Girls are different creatures," his father liked to tell him. "Once they get their claws deep under the skin, you'll be a goner."

This one, the girl on the front stoop, made eye contact with Vrable. Held the boy's gaze until that twinge of fear forced his eyes to the cement sidewalk in front of his new home.

"Just be nice and say hello to the girl," his mother prompted, once they were safe behind closed doors. "She's a darling little thing."

Two days later he saw her again, through the peephole in the door.

"She lives across the hall," his mother told him. "Stays with her grandmother, she does. She lost both parents, the poor dear."

How did they die? He didn't ask the question out loud, where anybody in the hallway might hear and become offended at his trespass into private matters that never will be any of his business. Was it a car wreck? Maybe they were both drug addicts who overdosed together. Perhaps they caught rabies from fruit bats that hide in the city, waiting to feed on the locals.

The next time Vrable saw the girl, she had returned to her perch on the front stoop. This time she wore a short red skirt that gave up a peek of her underwear—white, with little pink flowers.

"How come you're always staring at me?" she demanded from the boy.

Vrable stammered and stumbled over his own tongue, as if the thing had grown twelve feet in just the last minute. "I'm not *staring* at you," he protested.

"Liar, liar. . . I'm sure you know the rest."

His attempt to extract himself from the situation caught a snag when she asked his name.

"Vrable," he said.

"Vrable?" Indignation took up residence on her face. "What the heck kind of name is *Vrable?"*

"I'm named after an uncle," is all he could manage. "A great uncle, really; he died in Vietnam."

"Named after a dead man you never met, huh?"

"What's that got to do with anything?"

The girl ignored his question, remained in control of this conversation. "Your mom says you have a pony somewhere."

Vrable's head tipped forward. Girls like horses—or so he'd heard from Tommy Terwilliger. Tommy had been his best friend since they were both in kindergarten together. "His name is Ghost," he told the girl.

"What's up with you and the dead?"

Her question missed its mark, left him pondering her meaning.

She gained her feet, smoothed a wrinkle from her skirt, and clarified her curiosity. "You're named after a dead uncle—great uncle—and you have a pony called Ghost, which is a spirit of something that happens to be dead."

Vrable finally worked up enough nerve to ask the girl's name.

"Gotta go," is all she gave up.

It wasn't until their fourth encounter that she let slip the fact that she could still hear her mother's voice saying, "Worry changes nothing, Lucy. So don't waste time on such foolishness."

Vrable's laugh seemed misplaced.

"What's so funny?" the girl demanded.

"Your name is Lucy."

"And that's funny how?"

"Lucy Goosey." He only said it because it's a favorite saying of his father. *Everybody at the New Year's party was all loosey goosey by midnight.*

Lucy failed to see humor in the mocking of her name.

Vrable didn't set eyes on the girl for three whole days after that mistake. And he only deemed it a mistake because he found himself missing their odd conversations.

"Just knock on her door," his mother encouraged. "She most likely won't bite."

"Biting, I can handle." He found himself standing before the girl's apartment. It wasn't fear that kept him from laying knuckles to wood. It had more to do with curiosity. Like, wondering why he never saw Lucy's grandmother. And how come the old woman's voice didn't leak out into the hallway, the way everybody else's on that floor did?

"You come to make fun of me again?" Lucy had snuck up behind him. She wore red shorts and a pink t-shirt that said *Girl Power* in white letters across the front. "Wanna go down to the park?"

Did this constitute a date? No. They were just kids. But still, it would only be the two of them, alone, without parental supervision. Tommy Terwilliger would most certainly agree that this qualified as a legitimate date.

Lucy laid a squelch to those misguided thoughts. "And don't go thinking this is some kind of a date. It ain't."

His mother's voice invaded his head. *Ain't isn't a word.*

He'd let it slide this time.

The park really didn't resemble the mental picture he'd sketched. A more accurate label might be empty lot—or maybe the neighborhood dumping ground. A battered old sofa found use among the homeless few that chose to congregate in that spot. A pile of old tires lay at the rear of the space.

"Back behind the tires is the river," Lucy explained. "There's a place where we can sit and throw rocks in the water, if you want. Sometimes giant carp jump up, hoping what we're throwing can be eaten."

They found a place in a clearing. It was there that he picked up a scent on the girl—perfume of some sort. Did she splash it on because of him?

Side by side, they sat—close enough for their hips to touch. Stories of what brought each of them to this point in their lives found exchange like currency between them.

"Grandma really looks after me," Lucy said, tossing a small stone into the river. "I'd be stuck in foster if not for her."

"What's foster?" Vrable asked.

Her look reminded him of his own shortcomings. "You can't be that stupid," is all she said.

"I'd like to meet your grandmother," Vrable told her.

"Yeah, well, maybe. I don't know. Grandma hasn't been feeling well lately. She just needs her rest, is all."

He worked up the courage to toss those few words at her. "How'd your parents die?"

A giggle of sorts leaked from the girl. "They ain't really dead. I just told your mom that so she wouldn't keep asking after them. That's what grown-ups do—they dig and pry until they know everything about every kid on the block."

"Then where are they?" Vrable shot long glances from the side, hoped Lucy wasn't the kind of girl to just up and slug a boy for asking too many questions.

Lucy left out the giggle this time. Her shoulders did that quick flinch common to kids who don't have an answer for the question being asked. "Don't know," is all she said.

Once, way back when Vrable first got Ghost, he fell off the pony in mid-trot. The air evacuated his lungs and left the boy gasping in the dirt, searching for his breath. Lucy's confession struck him in the same way.

"Maybe you could ask the police to look for them," he offered, hopeful that resolution of her loss might be found.

Darkness settled into her slate-gray eyes. Anger, it may have been. Or perhaps resignation. The girl gained her feet, stood over top of the boy, as if ready to pounce. "You ever mention my name to a cop, I'll never talk to you again."

* * *

An entire week slipped by before Vrable caught sight of the girl again. This time he found her in the neighborhood grocery store, tossing items into a hand basket. Cereal, milk, cans of ravioli, and a pack of bubble gum.

Vrable's mom gave the boy a nudge, encouraged him to talk to the girl. "You don't just get up and walk away from a thing like losing your parents," Betty Tambor told her son. "A girl like her needs a friend."

"Yeah, well, maybe I know more than you do." He said it under his breath, knowing of a certainty he'd have to explain his meaning had he said it loud enough.

"Just grabbing some stuff," Lucy said, eyeing the boy and his mother. "Grandma doesn't get out much these days."

Betty Tambor spoke up, said, "Maybe you'll come to dinner at our place one of these evenings."

It wasn't really an invitation. It's just the way Vrable's mother speaks. She's always mingled that sort of vagueness with her words. Just float an idea out there, but don't ever really commit to it.

Lucy understood it, though. "Maybe," she said, injecting her own brand of vagueness into the breach. Her gaze fell to Vrable. "Wanna come over tonight?"

A shrug lifted off his shoulders like a spooked bird taking flight.

"Oh, go on over," his mother ordered. "It's Friday night. You may as well have some fun."

* * *

Lucy yanked her door wide open after only the first knock—as if she'd been there all day, just waiting for his visit.

The suddenness of it all gave Vrable a startle.

"Awful jumpy," she teased, inviting him inside. She wore that same red skirt again, the one offering free looks at her underwear whenever she sat on the front stoop.

Vrable wanted to look again.

"It's all in reverse," he said, absorbing the apartment's interior. "It's identical to ours, just in reverse."

"Then it's not identical," said Lucy, mingling a sort of sarcasm into her choice of words.

"Whatever." Vrable's backside found rest on a sofa that could have been there since the Reagan years. "Where's your grandma?"

"Out."

"Thought she didn't—"

"Leave it be, boy."

A bedroom door remained closed during his visit. Maybe that's where the old lady took her rest. The place lacked a television—though an outdated stereo occupied a shelf above the fake fireplace in the living room.

Lucy dropped beside the boy, leaving a few inches between them. Her scent hinted at something subtle, like a grown woman's perfume—one of those expensive brands his father used to buy his mother for Christmas or birthdays or anniversaries.

"What if I was a vampire," Lucy pondered, her gaze attached to his, "and I only invited you over to drain you?"

Vrable offered his neck to the girl. "Go ahead," he dared. "With my parents splitting up, there's not much left to look forward to."

The girl moved in closer. She didn't bite him, though; she just sniffed at his neck—as if determining whether or not he might be worth the effort.

"They'll get back together," she whispered into his ear. "And you'll move back to your home."

"No, they won't. You should see the way he looks at her now. He hates her."

"You're too young to appreciate real heartbreak, Vrable. Your father is more hurt than angry—don't ever confuse hurt with hatred."

Vrable fixed on her. "You're no older than me."

"Old enough to have seen more than *you've* seen."

It resembled a strawberry-colored butterfly, the birthmark adorning her left shoulder. His fingertips dared a touch. "Looks like a tattoo," he said, surprised by the sturdiness of his own voice.

Lucy's kiss came soft and lingering, sweetened by bubble gum. An unexpected thing, to be certain—not that the boy had it in mind to be offended by this sudden act. Even Tommy Terwilliger would be impressed—and Tommy isn't the easily impressed type.

"Why'd you do that?" he asked.

"Just felt like it," she replied.

The invitation leapt from his tongue before his wits had a chance to return. "Wanna come with me when I visit my dad this weekend?"

* * *

Vrable's mother gave him grief over not checking with her before asking Lucy to join him. "It's just common courtesy," she told him.

Mr. Tambor, he saw things through a different lens. "Got you a girlfriend, huh?" he asked, eyeing the girl climbing into the back of his car.

Vrable denied such a concept—though Lucy's kiss remained on his lips these many days later. "She's just a friend," he claimed, not truly believing his own words.

"Different creatures," said Mr. Tambor, wiggling his fingers at his son. "Claws, I tell ya."

Small talk filled the car ride out of Brooklyn. Mr. Tambor spoke of goings-on out in the country. He brought Vrable up to date on news about neighbors and other locals. Lucy, she kept mostly quiet in the back seat, though every so often she'd toss in a stray word or two where a subject stood neutral, not wrapped around people and places of which she knew nothing.

"This is all yours?" she asked, eyeing the expanse of fields surrounding the Tambor home.

"Two hundred acres," Vrable proclaimed with pride.

His father tucked a few words into the seams of the moment, said, "And it's all going to be yours one day, Son."

They wasted little time getting to the old barn, Vrable and Lucy.

"It's over a hundred years old," Vrable said, meaning the barn. "My great grandfather built it—with the help of some Amish people."

The smell of hay and manure mingled around them. It didn't seem to bother Lucy—not the way it often bothered other girls he'd known from school. But then again, there weren't any girls like Lucy at Vrable's old school.

"What's that for?" she asked, eyeing the brood lamp in the corner.

"It's for when we have baby chicks," he explained. "It keeps them warm during cold nights."

A fascination, he'd call it, the girl's interest in such a normal thing like a brood lamp.

She turned it on, turned it off, turned it back on again. "I thought the mother is supposed to keep them warm."

"Sometimes she needs help."

And just that quick, Lucy lost interest. "Where's Ghost?"

They found the pony grazing in the pasture behind the barn. Ghost let go a whinny and trotted toward the boy. It's joy that passed between the two—an honest and certain thing. They'd been separated by time and miles, sure, but still retained the familiarity of old friends—or even family.

"Can we ride him?" Lucy asked.

Saddle and bridle found the animal more than willing. Vrable mounted first, before pulling his guest up behind him. A gentle kick set Ghost on a steady walk toward an open field.

Lucy's arms went easily around Vrable. She hugged tight to the boy, as if she might fall off at any moment. It's a thing like comfort—that feeling he got being so close to her. He could imagine her living there with him. After all, the farm would be his one day, thus securing his right to choose who could stay there with him.

For dinner, Mr. Tambor made hot dogs and macaroni and cheese—a long-time favorite of Vrable's. Plans were discussed as to what father and son might do with their limited time together. Both opted for fishing in the small lake just down the road.

"Fishing?" Lucy's nose crinkled at the notion.

Mr. Tambor asked, "Ever been?"

"Nope." The girl scratched at that strawberry butterfly on her arm. "Can't I just stay here with Ghost?"

"Girls like horses," Vrable offered, hoping to sound as wise as Tommy Terwilliger. "Ghost will keep her company."

* * *

"I hate the city," Vrable confessed to his father after casting his line into the lake. "It's loud and dirty and just not home."

"Well…" Mr. Tambor couldn't furnish a ready solution—and Vrable hadn't really expected one. "Things get complicated, Son. But they always have a way of untangling themselves if we just remain patient."

Neither caught any fish worth keeping. They rarely did. But that's never been the purpose of lazy afternoons on the lake.

"Think you'll ever forgive her?" It was a bold move on Vrable's part, asking such a question. But his father, well, he wasn't given to flying off the handle over things his boy did or said.

Mr. Tambor retrieved a handkerchief from his back pocket, wiped the sweat from his forehead, and settled his gaze on Vrable. "How'd you ever get to be so darn smart?"

That's all he said.

There wouldn't be any deep conversations regarding infidelity in marriage or the pain of a broken heart. Those were the things adults kept for themselves, like secrets saved in a box, visited only on rare occasions, when the one feeling the pain is certain he's all alone. A kid, well, he never knows what happened until after the family splinters, its members falling into different places in the world.

It wasn't until the sun dipped beneath the horizon that Vrable noticed the orange glow painting the sky toward home.

"What's *that?*" he asked.

* * *

Vrable saw it first. Flames from the barn licked the evening sky, became visible a mile away.

Ghost became an afterthought.

"Lucy!" the boy screamed, jumping from his father's car before the thing had a chance to become motionless. He bolted toward the conflagration.

Mr. Tambor tackled him in the space between the house and barn. "If she's in there, it's too late, Vrable."

Kicking, fighting, and growling did little to break his father's hold. All he could do was watch.

Ancient timbers gave way beneath the heat, dropping the roof upon the wreckage. Within minutes the walls folded, no longer willing or able to do what they'd been doing for over a hundred years.

Movement beyond the smoke put Ghost safely in the pasture.

The girl, she failed to show.

Even a desperate search of the house and surrounding fields couldn't locate her.

Fire trucks lined the long driveway; hoses lay here and there across the lawn. Only a pile of rubble remained once the flames were extinguished.

Vrable's mother arrived as the firemen sifted the remains in their search for Lucy. The usual harsh tone between both parents had gone soft in the shadow of current events.

"You'll stay out here tonight?" Mr. Tambor asked his estranged wife.

Her head tipped a reluctant nod.

* * *

"She wasn't in the barn," a firefighter reported.

Vrable saw a positive in this finding. "Maybe she got scared and ran to catch the train back home."

Relieved to know this, Mr. Tambor asked, "Any idea what started this thing?"

"Too soon to be certain," the fireman explained, "but it's looking like your brood lamp got things going."

Attitudes changed that night—at least where Vrable's parents were concerned. Anger and mistrust gave way to feelings neither parent had given much thought to in recent years. At dawn's first light, Betty Tambor found her kitchen just as she'd left it months earlier. Morning put the family back together at the breakfast table.

"We have to go find Lucy," Vrable demanded, refusing the plate of scrambled eggs set before him.

His father said, "The police—"

"Lucy doesn't want the police to even know her name," Vrable argued. "Can't we just go to Brooklyn and see if she made it home?"

They drove to the city together, as a family—for the first time in a long while.

* * *

Vrable darted up the front walk, hoping he just might find the girl at her usual perch atop the steps.

No such luck.

The boy bolted up the stairs to their floor, well ahead of his parents. His frantic banging at the door belonging to

Lucy and her grandmother brought out the curious from the other apartments on the floor.

The building super opened the door, demanded to know just what Vrable thought he was doing making such a ruckus.

"Is she here?" Vrable asked, gulping at the air for needed breath.

The super eyed the boy like he'd gone soft in the head. "Is *who* here?"

"Lucy!"

"There's no Lucy staying here."

"Then what about her grandma?"

Mr. and Mrs. Tambor entered the scene, attempted to calm the boy.

"She's not here," Vrable told them through words thickened by emotion.

Betty Tambor offered her input. "A small girl," she explained, "dark hair, freckles. She stays here with her grandmother."

The super's head wagged left to right. "There's nobody staying in this unit."

Betty said, "But surely her grandmother would—"

"As I said, this one is vacant. Has been for more than two months." He pushed the door open, showed off an empty space under remodel.

* * *

Vrable and his mother settled back on the farm just in time for the start of the new school year. Anger had subsided, the hurt his father endured softened. Bitterness became sweetened by the news that Vrable would have a younger sibling by the following spring.

Prenatal doctor visits took place in Brooklyn, a few short blocks from the apartment. Vrable referred to that chapter in time as *the separation.* He did what he could to leave those unfortunate few months in the past, rarely recalling them aloud—unless Tommy Terwilliger pestered the boy with questions. Tommy hadn't spent much time in the city. He appreciated details—mostly those concerning Lucy.

"I can't tell you what happened to her because I just don't know," Vrable often told his friend.

"Just vanished, huh? Like a ghost?"

But then Vrable saw her again, a few days before Christmas, outside Dr. Rudcliff's office. She'd changed considerably, this one. Taller. Older—by more than a few years. Twenty—if she were a day. Same face, though. That strawberry butterfly on her left shoulder capped it. Who wears short sleeves in a New York winter?

"Hey!" Vrable called to her.

Her eyes fixed on him, like maybe she really didn't recognize the boy she now towered over. She said, "What do you want, kid?"

Vrable lost his words behind an emotion he fought to keep in check.

"So. . ." she said, drifting into his orbit. "Cat got. . . well, you know the rest."

"You're Lucy." The boy's voice carried the heavy weight of a tremble behind it.

"And you're Vrable. Named after a dead great-uncle." In a moment, buried in a piece of time thin as a slip of paper, Lucy stood as the ten-year-old girl she'd previously been. "You want me like this, do you? Easier for you to relate to?"

A thing like that could startle a boy, make him question his own eyes—if not his very sanity.

He grasped at words, managed to string a few together. "What are you?"

She leaned in close to the boy, her lips brushed his ear. Warmth filled her tone. "I'm just a friend, Vrable."

The salt of tears stung his eyes. "Then why did you leave?"

"I didn't." Her arms went easily around him, pulled him close in a hug. "You just stopped seeing me."

"I don't understand."

Lucy backed away. Her fingers caressed the boy's cheek. "I told you they'd get back together," she said.

The girl disappeared from the very spot on which she stood. She didn't walk away, didn't run off. She simply ceased to be there in front of him.

"You're going to have a sister," Vrable's mother said, finding him out front of Dr. Rudcliff's office.

Though Lucy had vanished, Vrable could still feel her near him—her warmth, her scent lingering as if she'd just stepped behind him. "Do you believe in angels?" he asked his mother.

The woman pondered her son, considered his question. "I suppose I do—though I sometimes wonder where they are when so many people seem to need them."

"Maybe they're not meant to be like superheroes," he countered, following his mother back to the car. "Maybe they show up just to sort of untangle things." He climbed into the passenger seat, clicked his seatbelt, said, "Can we name her Lucy?"

About Beem Weeks

Beem Weeks is the author of short stories, poems, essays, and novels. Among his literary influences he counts Daniel Woodrell, Barbara Kingsolver, and Stephen Geez. A pop-culture trivia buff, Beem's passions include indie films, loud music, and a well-told story. He has also penned a collection of short stories entitled *Slivers of Life* and the novel *Jazz Baby*.

Fresh Ink Group

Independent Publisher

ᴓ

Hardcovers
Softcovers
All Ebook Platforms
Worldwide Distribution

ᴓ

Indie Author Services
Book Development, Editing, Proofing
Graphic/Cover Design
Video/Trailer Production
Website Creation
Social Media Management
Writing Contests
Writers' Blogs
Podcasts

ᴓ

Authors
Editors
Artists
Experts
Professionals

ᴓ

FreshInkGroup.com
Email: info@FreshInkGroup.com
Twitter: @FreshInkGroup
Facebook.com/FreshInkGroup
LinkedIn: Fresh Ink Group

While all of Mississippi bakes in the scorching summer of 1925, sudden orphanhood wraps its icy embrace around pretty Emily Ann "Baby" Teegarten, a young teen.

Taken in by an aunt bent on ridding herself of this unexpected burden, Baby Teegarten plots her escape using the only means at her disposal: a voice that brings church ladies to righteous tears, and makes both angels and devils take notice.

"I'm going to New York City to sing jazz," she brags to anybody who'll listen. But the Big Apple, well, it's an awful long way from that dry patch of earth she'd always called home.

So when the smoky stages of New Orleans speakeasies give a whistle, offering all sorts of shortcuts, Emily Ann soon learns it's the whorehouses and opium dens that can sidetrack a girl and dim a spotlight...and knowing the wrong people can snuff it out.

Jazz Baby
just wants to sing–
not fight to stay alive.

20 short stories peek into individual lives caught up in spectacular moments in time. Children, teens, mothers, and the elderly each have stories to share. Witness tragedy and fulfillment, love and hate, loss and renewal. Historical events become backdrops in the lives of ordinary people, those souls forgotten with the passage of time. Diverse issues run the gamut from Alzheimer's disease to civil rights, abandonment to abuse, from young love to the death of a child. Long-hidden secrets and notions of revenge unfold at the promptings of rich and realistic characters; plot lines often lead readers into strange and dark corners. Within Slivers of Life, everybody has a story to tell—and no two are ever exactly alike.

www.ingramcontent.com/pod-product-compliance
Lightning Source LLC
Chambersburg PA
CBHW071003180726
48291CB00004B/1410